50 Walks in
KENT

First published 2002
Researched and written by Rebecca Ford

Produced by AA Publishing
© Automobile Association Developments Limited 2002
Illustrations © Automobile Association Developments Limited 2002
Reprinted 2004

Published by AA Publishing (a trading name of Automobile
Association Developments Limited, whose registered office is
Millstream, Maidenhead, Windsor, SL4 5GD;
registered number 1878835).

Ordnance Survey® This product includes mapping data licensed from
Ordnance Survey® with the permission of the
Controller of Her Majesty's Stationery Office.
© Crown copyright 2004. All rights reserved. Licence number 399221

ISBN 0 7495 3333 1

A CIP catalogue record for this book is available
from the British Library.

The contents of this book are believed correct at the time of printing.
Nevertheless, the publishers cannot be held responsible for any errors
or omissions or for changes in the details given in this book or for
the consequences of any reliance on the information it provides. This
does not affect your statutory rights. We have tried to ensure
accuracy in this book, but things do change and we would be grateful
if readers would advise us of any inaccuracies they may encounter.

We have taken all reasonable steps to ensure that these walks are
safe and achievable by walkers with a realistic level of fitness.
However, all outdoor activities involve a degree of risk and the
publishers accept no responsibility for any injuries caused to
readers whilst following these walks. For more advice on walking
safely see page 128. The mileage range shown on the front cover is for
guidance only – some walks may exceed or be less than these
distances.

Visit the AA Publishing website at www.theAA.com

Paste-up and editorial by Outcrop Publishing Services Ltd, Cumbria
for AA Publishing

A02038

Printed in Italy by G Canale & C SPA, Torino, Italy

Legend

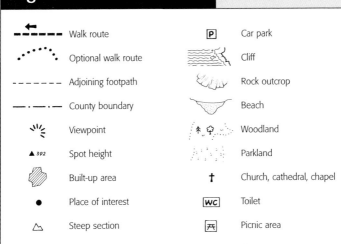

← - - - - -	Walk route	🅿	Car park
⋅⋅⋅⋅⋅⋅	Optional walk route	〜〜〜	Cliff
- - - - - -	Adjoining footpath		Rock outcrop
— ⋅ — ⋅ —	County boundary	▽	Beach
☼	Viewpoint	♣ ♧	Woodland
▲ 392	Spot height		Parkland
🔲	Built-up area	†	Church, cathedral, chapel
●	Place of interest	WC	Toilet
△	Steep section	🏕	Picnic area

Kent locator map

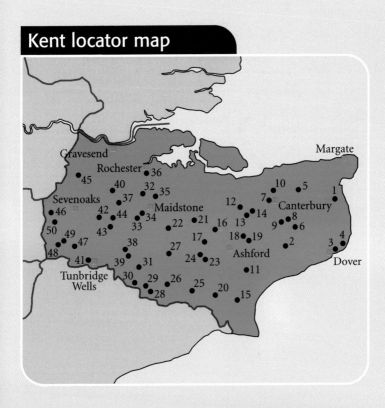

Contents

Contents

Rating: Each walk is rated for its relative difficulty compared to the other walks in this book. Walks marked 🚶🚶 🚶🚶 🚶🚶 are likely to be shorter and easier with little total ascent. The hardest walks are marked 🚶🚶 🚶🚶 🚶🚶 .

Walking in Safety: For advice and safety tips ➤ 128.

Introducing Kent

It was early morning and a thick mist was rising from the hidden hollows of the Kentish Weald, curling its wispy fingers around the branches of ancient trees, and then stretching them slowly into the sky. From my position high on the chalky scarp of the North Downs, I watched as the warm red roof of an oast house peered sleepily through the haze. It was soon followed by the spire of a church, then a dense tangle of woodland – and eventually the distant sparkle of a stream. Soon the whole of the Weald was spread out before me.

Walking in Kent is full of moments like this. But while vast numbers of people come here each year, few bother to stop and explore – most simply travel through as fast as possible, in their haste to get from London to the Channel ports. In fact Kent is often seen as little more than a southerly extension of the capital. Yet the county has a character that is all its own, with an extraordinary

diversity of landscapes and deliciously rich history. And since it has over 4,200 miles (6,758km) of public rights of way to explore, the best way to see it is on foot.

Of course there are large urban areas, and an inordinate number of busy roads and motorways; but much of the county still has a rural flavour. The scenery is so fine that a third of Kent is officially designated an Area of Outstanding Natural Beauty. The landscape is also very varied. To the north are the Downs, the uplands that run through Kent like a long, chalky spine; to the south is the High Weald, an area of wild woodland and rolling hills. The coastline is different again, a delicate ribbon of dramatic cliffs, sandy beaches and mysterious marshlands. And sprinkled liberally through this ancient landscape are orchards, oast houses, hop gardens and villages – which are impossibly photogenic with their weatherboarded cottages, duck ponds, traditional inns and sleepy churchyards. This could be quintessential rural England.

The county is steeped in history, for this is the land where the Saxons first landed, where the Normans built their first castles and over which the Battle of Britain was fought. At Charing, you can follow the Pilgrims' Way, the age-old pathway used by generations of travellers; at Aylesford and Trottiscliffe you can walk tracks punctuated by ancient burial mounds. There are memories of smugglers on Romney Marshes, of the Romans at Eynsford and of Henry VIII at Hever. And literary links are everywhere. You can walk with Chaucer's pilgrims in

---

PUBLIC TRANSPORT ⓘ

There are frequent train services between the main towns and cities in Kent and central London (such as Rochester, Walk 36; Canterbury, Walk 7 and Tunbridge Wells, Walk 41). However, do remember that these are commuter services and get exceptionally crowded during peak hours. Travel within Kent by train is not so simple and may involve some changes of train. All trains are liable to cancellation at very short notice. For rail information call National Rail Enquiries on 08457 48 49 50. If you wish to use local buses you will have to plan very carefully as services vary throughout the county. Bus information is provided by Traveline 0870 608 2608.

Canterbury, see the house where Jane Austen wrote *Pride and Prejudice*, or walk the streets of Rochester with Charles Dickens. You don't have to travel far from a busy motorway to feel that you have discovered an earlier England, a land of bluebell woods, sunken lanes, flower-drenched meadows and tranquil river valleys.

Kent is laced with long distance footpaths. There's the Eden Valley Walk linking Edenbridge and Tonbridge; the Medway Valley Walk between Tonbridge and Rochester; the Saxon Shore Way, stretching 163 miles (262km) around the coast, and the High Weald Walk, encircling Tunbridge Wells. Then there's the Greensand Way, a trail of 108 miles (174km) along the Greensand ridge; the High Weald Landscape Trail; the Elham Valley Way; the Stour Valley Walk and, of course, the North Downs Way, following the Pilgrims' Way between Farnham and Dover. All of these trails can be linked with other footpaths to make circular walks – frequently dotted with traditional tea shops and cosy pubs. Kent's got so much to offer that once you start walking you just won't want to stop.

Using this Book

Information panels
An information panel for each walk shows its relative difficulty (➤ 5), the distance and total amount of ascent. An indication of the gradients you will encounter is shown by the rating 🞀🞀🞀 (no steep slopes) to 🞀🞀🞀 (several very steep slopes).

Maps
There are 30 maps, covering 40 of the walks. Some walks have a suggested option in the same area. The information panel for these walks will tell you how much extra walking is involved. On short-cut suggestions the panel will tell you the total distance if you set out from the start of the main walk. Where an option returns to the same point on the main walk, just the distance of the loop is given. Where an option leaves the main walk at one point and returns to it at another, then the distance shown is for the whole walk. The minimum time suggested is for reasonably fit walkers and doesn't allow for stops. Each walk has a suggested map. Laminated aqua3 maps are longer lasting and water resistant.

Start Points
The start of each walk is given as a six-figure grid reference prefixed by two letters indicating which 100km square of the National Grid it refers to. You'll find more information on grid references on most Ordnance Survey maps.

Dogs
We have tried to give dog owners useful advice about how dog friendly each walk is. Please respect other countryside users. Keep your dog under control, especially around livestock, and obey local bylaws and other dog control notices.

Car Parking
Many of the car parks suggested are public, but occasionally you may find you have to park on the roadside or in a lay-by. Please be considerate when you leave your car, ensuring that access roads or gates are not blocked and that other vehicles can pass safely.

A Taste of Sandwich

A gentle trail around this picturesque town.

•DISTANCE•	3 miles (4.8km)
•MINIMUM TIME•	1hr 30min
•ASCENT / GRADIENT•	98ft (30m) ▲▲▲
•LEVEL OF DIFFICULTY•	🚶 🚶 🚶
•PATHS•	Easy town streets and field tracks, 9 stiles
•LANDSCAPE•	Impossibly quaint townscape surrounded by salt flats
•SUGGESTED MAP•	aqua3 OS Explorer 150 Canterbury & the Isle of Thanet
•START / FINISH•	Grid reference: TR 351582
•DOG FRIENDLINESS•	Pretty good, can run free in some sections
•PARKING•	Behind Guildhall in Sandwich
•PUBLIC TOILETS•	New Street, Sandwich

BACKGROUND TO THE WALK

As you walk around Sandwich, you can't help but be struck by the town's picturesque appearance. With its half-timbered houses and historic churches, it has a quiet English charm, the sort that makes you think of tea and scones and Thora Hird. It's hard to imagine these narrow streets echoing with the footsteps of raiders, smugglers and pirates. Yet Sandwich was once the most important port in England – the Dover of its day – and was one of the original Cinque Ports.

Strategic Ports

The Cinque Ports (pronounced 'sink') was the name given to the confederation of five (later seven) important ports on the south east coast that guarded England in the days before there was an official navy. Hastings, New Romney, Dover, Hythe and Sandwich, together with Rye and Winchelsea, were important fishing and trading centres. This meant they had plenty of men and ships that the King could press into service, whether he wanted free transport to Europe for his family or a force to repel invaders. It was convenient for the monarch – and in those days no one was going to argue. Sandwich was of particular importance as it occupied a strategic position on the coast, and was frequently raided by both the Danes and the French.

The tradition began with the early Saxons and was well established by the time of Edward the Confessor (*c*1003–1066), who made use of Cinque Port ships. By the 13th century, the towns had become so important to England that they were formally granted certain rights and privileges. These included freedom from taxes and customs duties, certain trading concessions, and even their own courts and punishments. In return, each town had to supply a quota of men and ships whenever the monarch required. It was a pretty good deal and provided plenty of opportunity for local merchants and traders to make money. The Cinque Ports consequently became some of the richest and most powerful centres in Europe.

The quay at Sandwich, now so quiet, would have bustled in those days as fighting men embarked for Europe, and ships laden with valuable cargoes of silks, spices and wine were unloaded. It would have been intimidating too, for smugglers and pirates operated from here, attracted by the rich pickings on offer. All the ports had a violent reputation. However, their power and influence was not to last. A terrible storm in 1287 permanently altered the coastline. The sea began to retreat and the harbour at Sandwich, and other ports, eventually became so choked with silt they could no longer be used. After a permanent navy was established the privileges of the Cinque Ports were revoked and Sandwich sank back into relative obscurity.

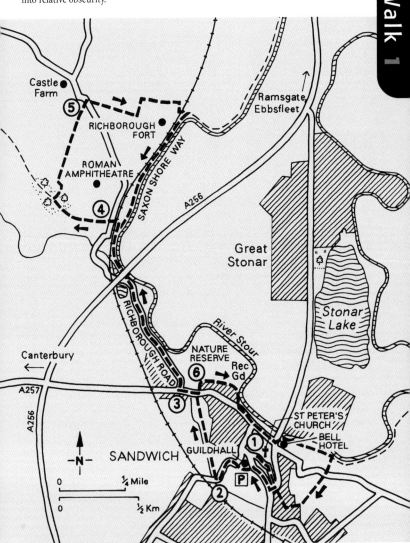

Walk 1 **Directions**

① From **St Peter's Church** in the centre of the town, walk down **St Peter's Street** to **The Chain**. Turn right into **Galliard Street**, walk to **New Street** and continue to the Guildhall. Go left, through the car park and up to the **Rope Walk**, where rope makers used this long, straight area to lay out their ropes.

② Turn right and when you reach the road, cross over and turn right down **The Butts**. At the main road turn left, cross over and turn right up **Richborough Road**.

③ Walk ahead, past a scrapyard, and go through a gate to join a footpath on the right. Follow the track round, under the main road and up to the railway line. Nip over the stile and cross the line with care, then go over two more stiles and on to the road.

> **WHAT TO LOOK FOR** ⓘ
> **Richborough Fort** was once the gateway to Roman Britain. Claudius' legions landed here in AD 43 before launching their invasion and you can still see their defensive ditches. Known as Rutupiae by the Romans, the fort guarded what was then the main port of entry to Britain. Inside you can see a large masonry cross dating back to AD 80, which is thought to commemorate the conquest.

④ Cross over, go over another stile, then walk across the field to the trees, heading for the third telegraph pole. The path now plunges into the wood and up a wide track. Where it splits, fork right and go through the trees to a stile. Now follow the fence line and two more stiles over a couple of fields to join the road.

⑤ Cross over and walk up the track ahead. **Richborough Fort** is ahead. The path runs around the fort with expansive views over this seemingly endless landscape. At the bottom of the track turn right along the end of a garden. Nip over the stile and back over the railway, leaving it by another stile. The path now leads to the right, over a rather neglected looking lock and back beside the river. You will eventually rejoin the

> **WHILE YOU'RE THERE** ⓘ
> At **Ebbsfleet**, a couple of miles from Sandwich, is the spot where the Jutes, Hengist and Horsa, are said to have landed their longships in AD 449. They and their troops quickly took control of Kent, which became the first Anglo-Saxon kingdom. The English nation was effectively born here.

road, and retrace your steps to the end of **Richborough Road** where you turn left.

⑥ Go left through a kissing gate, pass the **Nature Reserve** and go round the edge of a recreation ground. Turn right through a gate, come on to **Strand Street** and turn left. Go left in front of the **Bell Hotel**, and right past the Barbican. Walk along the riverbank, following the line of the old town wall. At a bend in the river, turn right to a road. Cross over, continue along the footpath, pass the bowling green, then turn right down steps into **Mill Wall Place**. Cross over and go back along **King Street** to the start.

> **WHERE TO EAT AND DRINK** ⓘ
> There is plenty of choice in Sandwich, which has a good mix of tea shops, pubs and restaurants. The **New Inn** on Delf Street serves hot drinks, soup, sandwiches and light meals such as baked potatoes.

In Search of Elham's Secret Stream

A varied walk through open countryside that takes you over an elusive stream and up to a hidden church.

•DISTANCE•	3½ miles (5.7km)
•MINIMUM TIME•	1hr 45min
•ASCENT / GRADIENT•	115ft (35m) ▲▲▲
•LEVEL OF DIFFICULTY•	👫 👫 👫
•PATHS•	Well-marked field tracks and footpaths, 9 stiles
•LANDSCAPE•	Fertile fields and lush green valley
•SUGGESTED MAP•	aqua3 OS Explorer 138 Dover, Folkestone & Hythe
•START / FINISH•	Grid reference: TR 177438
•DOG FRIENDLINESS•	Dogs on lead through grazed areas
•PARKING•	By Elham church
•PUBLIC TOILETS•	None on route

BACKGROUND TO THE WALK

Although you'll cross the course of the Nail Bourne on both the outward and return legs of this walk, the chances are that you won't be aware of it – for this is Kent's most elusive stream and it only flows in the wettest winters. The waters (bourne is an old local word for stream) used to be known as the Woe Waters, for their flow was once believed to herald death or disaster.

Battle of the Gods

The Nail Bourne has strong associations with the conversion of Kent to Christianity. Although some Britons became Christians during the Roman occupation (AD 43–406), the country gradually returned to paganism when the Romans left. When St Augustine came to this part of England in AD 597 to convert the Anglo-Saxons to Christianity, the county had experienced an extended period of drought. Crops had failed, animals had died and the local people began to feel that their interest in this new religion had offended their pagan gods. The Christian priests, sensing trouble, hastily began to pray for rain. Legend has it that, on the spot where St Augustine knelt to pray, a spring miraculously – and conveniently – appeared and flowed through what is now the Elham Valley. Furious at this display of Christian power, the pagan gods were said to have dried the stream, which God, just as promptly, made flow again.

This supernatural struggle is said to explain why the stream still disappears in dry weather. In fact, the Nail Bourne is an example of a winterbourne – a seasonal stream that is a distinctive feature of chalklands. They occur because chalk is porous and rain quickly seeps down through it and disappears from view. However, if there is a thick layer of clay further down, a spring develops. This spring will only turn into a stream if it is extremely wet – so winterbournes appear and disappear as if by magic. The wildlife that lives in these streams is especially adapted to survive drought, then reproduce and colonise rapidly as soon as water returns.

'They Seek Him Here, They Seek Him There…'

Just as mysterious as the Nail Bourne was the 'dammed elusive' Scarlet Pimpernel, the fictional character who saved so many French aristocrats from the guillotine. It is said that the man on whom Baroness Orczy (1865–1947) modelled her swashbuckling hero, used to stop at the Rose and Crown, an old staging post in Elham, before galloping off on his way to France to save real life aristocrats from the revolutionaries. The Baroness, a Hungarian who settled in the Kent village of Bearsted, was a slightly eccentric character. She liked to travel around in a coach and four, and expected local people to show their respect by curtseying or doffing their caps. If they didn't she would react by throwing an undignified tantrum.

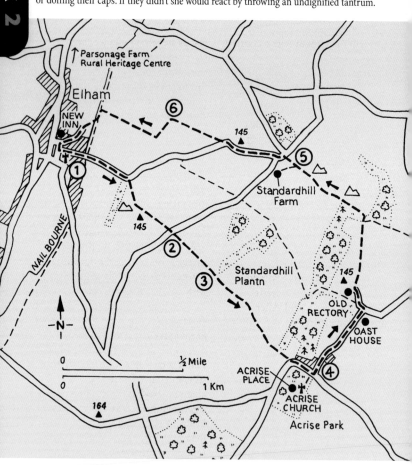

Walk 2 Directions

① From the church walk down **Duck Street**, then head uphill to a footpath on the right. Cross the stile and continue uphill, then nip over another stile at the top of the field.

Walk straight ahead and cross two more stiles to the road.

② Cross here and follow the footpath ahead, through a gate, then along the field edge – if it's just been ploughed you'll see plenty of flints exposed. The path goes downhill, and into the next field past a pylon.

③ Go past a small wood, through a gate and follow the guide posts over the next field. Cross another stile into an army training area, then walk around a wood. Go straight over to a yellow marker by a stile, on to a road and up to the crossroads (you can make a detour through the trees to Acrise church).

WHERE TO EAT AND DRINK ⓘ

The **New Inn** at Elham is a friendly pub, whose owners are happy to make you a pot of tea after your walk and are amazingly tolerant of muddy boots. In winter there's a small wood burning stove to snuggle round.

---

④ Otherwise turn left and continue until you pass an old oast house. Turn left just after this, then take the right-hand path to the **Old Rectory**, signed 'Private Road'. Go over a stile immediately in front of the house, then cross a meadow. After a gate your route leads diagonally over a field. After another gate, turn left and walk along a field edge. After another gate the path goes steeply downhill. The path now descends steeply to

---

WHAT TO LOOK FOR ⓘ

The **Church of St Mary the Virgin** in Elham is well worth a look. It dates back to 1180 and has some unusual 19th-century stained glass, in which contemporary figures are portrayed as characters from the Bible. Look closely and you'll see Thomas Carlyle, William Gladstone and Benjamin Disraeli.

---

the valley bottom, then rises again, just as steeply, to join a concrete track up to the farm. Where the track bears left, you go right and through a gate and up to the farm buildings. Go through a rather rusty gate and turn left when you reach the road.

⑤ At the house turn right and go along the road under a line of pylons. Just after a copse the lane bears left. Go ahead down a footpath and then downhill along the edge of a field. Walk across another field following the clearly marked path and at the bottom left-hand corner go over a stile with a rather a long drop.

⑥ Head along the edge of the field, keeping the fence on your right. Follow the fence and at the corner follow it downhill and over another stile. After another field go left along the field edge. You'll come to a gate which takes you over a stone bridge. Walk diagonally across the field in the direction of the church. One more gate brings you up to a lane and back to the **church**.

WHILE YOU'RE THERE ⓘ

At North Elham, a short distance away, you can visit **Parsonage Farm Rural Heritage Centre**. It has many rare breeds of farm animals, including several types of sheep. There are displays on wool and cereal production, as well as ancient crafts such as hedge laying.

Butterflies Over Dover

An exhilarating trail over Dover's famous white cliffs.

•DISTANCE•	5½ miles (8.8km)
•MINIMUM TIME•	2hrs 30min
•ASCENT / GRADIENT•	131ft (40m) ▲▲▲
•LEVEL OF DIFFICULTY•	🚶🚶 🚶🚶 🚶🚶
•PATHS•	Chalky cliff paths, some sections of road
•LANDSCAPE•	Grassy clifftops with extensive sea views
•SUGGESTED MAP•	aqua3 OS Explorer 138 Dover, Folkestone & Hythe
•START / FINISH•	Grid reference: TR 321412
•DOG FRIENDLINESS•	Good, but best to start from clifftop car park with a dog
•PARKING•	Russell Street and St James Lane, also on cliffs by National Trust tea room
•PUBLIC TOILETS•	Dover and National Trust tea room

BACKGROUND TO THE WALK

Go on, admit it. As soon as you saw that this walk took you over those famous white cliffs you came over all Vera Lynn and hummed, 'There'll be bluebirds over the white cliffs of Dover,' to yourself. It's okay, practically everyone who walks here does the same at some point. Yet while this distinctive landmark is known all over the world and is seen as a symbol of England, few people realise that it is also an important wildlife habitat – so important that it supports species that are rarely found elsewhere in the country.

The Chalk Downland

The cliffs, which are made of chalk, are topped with a thin, porous soil that has been grazed by animals for hundreds of years, creating what is known as chalk downland. Grazing stops coarse grasses and scrub invading the land and creates the ideal environment for hundreds of wild flowers to flourish. And while the early farmers didn't realise it, they were creating unique plant communities. While you're walking, keep your eyes peeled for plants like horseshoe vetch, early spider orchid and yellow rattle that gets its name from the seed pods that rattle in the wind. And with wild flowers, of course, come butterflies – particularly those wonderful blue ones that you so rarely see these days. Look out for the silvery chalkhill blue and the gorgeous sapphire Adonis blue. I even spotted a butterfly here in December. It wasn't close enough to identify, but it was a cheering sight nonetheless.

Grazing Ponies

Other wild creatures of the cliffs include adders (you're unlikely to see one, they hide from people), slow worms (not a snake but a legless lizard), common lizards and birds such as fulmars, peregrine falcons and skylarks – no bluebirds though.

Unfortunately modern farming methods have led to a 98 per cent decline in chalk downland and with it, of course, a similar decline in the plants and animals it supports. In an attempt to halt this decline, the National Trust has introduced Exmoor ponies to the white cliffs. These hardy little ponies eat the coarse grasses that would otherwise invade the land, and so allow the wild flowers to grow.

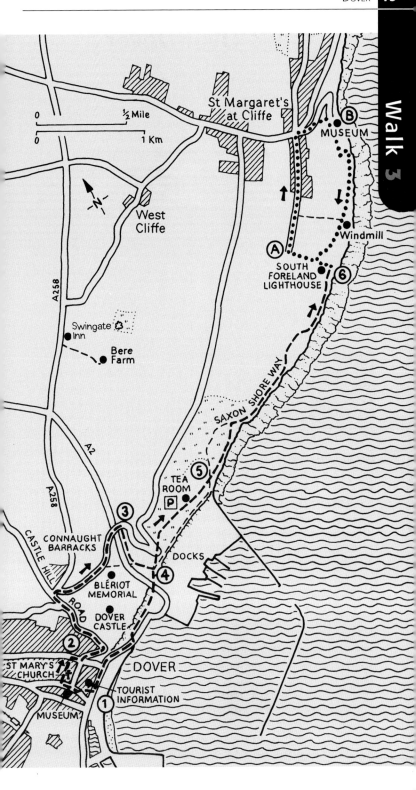

St Margaret's at Cliffe

MUSEUM Ⓑ

West Cliffe

A258

Windmill

Ⓐ

SOUTH FORELAND LIGHTHOUSE

Ⓐ

Ⓑ

Swingate Inn

Bere Farm

SAXON SHORE WAY

A2

TEA ROOM
Ⓟ

Ⓢ

A258

Ⓒ

CONNAUGHT BARRACKS

Ⓓ

DOCKS

BLÉRIOT MEMORIAL

CASTLE HILL ROAD

DOVER CASTLE

Ⓑ

ST MARY'S CHURCH

DOVER

TOURIST INFORMATION

Ⓐ

MUSEUM

0   ½ Mile

0   1 Km

N

Walk 3

Walk 3 Directions

① From the **tourist information centre** on the front, walk to the right and at a roundabout go up **Bench Street**. At a crossing turn left into the market square. **Dover Museum** is just to the left. Turn up the road on the right. Keep going to **St Mary's Church** and then turn right along the path that runs beside the church. Keep ahead through the car park, cross some water and come out on to **Maison Dieu Road**.

> ### WHILE YOU'RE THERE
> **Dover Castle** was built by the Normans after the Conquest in 1066 to control the native population. But the site, high above the sea, has an even more ancient history. There was an Iron-Age hill fort here and the Romans used the site to defend this part of their empire. Inside the castle you can see the remains of the Pharos, a beacon, which helped to guide the Roman fleet into the harbour.

② Turn right here, and then left, steeply, up **Castle Hill Road**. Eventually pass the entrance to **Dover Castle**. Further on, just past **Connaught Barracks**, turn right along Upper Road, signed 'Blériot Memorial'.

③ Cross the bridge over the main road and then take the footpath on the right. Go down some steps, fork left and, in a few paces, fork right.

Continue on this track and eventually emerge from the scrub to see the sea.

④ Turn left here, walk up some steps, with docks on your right. At a National Trust car park follow the **Saxon Shore Way** down to the right and over the cliffs. Continue past the coastguard station to a gate.

⑤ The path now continues along the cliffs and up to **South Foreland Lighthouse**. Some of the tracks branch off and lead very close to the cliffs – but there is a danger of cliff falls so keep to the main route. You may see some Exmoor ponies on this part of the walk. They've been introduced to the cliffs to graze the rare chalk downland and help preserve the habitat.

⑥ At **South Foreland Lighthouse** turn around and retrace your steps along the cliff – no hardship when you have these views. You can take the upper path here and walk past the **National Trust tea room** if you fancy stopping for tea. Otherwise continue down the steps and walk under the main road. Go along **Athol Terrace**, past the **First and Last** pub, and up on to the main road and back to the start point.

> ### WHERE TO EAT AND DRINK
> The **National Trust tea room** on the cliffs is the best place to stop. You can get tea, scones and cakes or something more substantial, like a hot sandwich.

> ### WHAT TO LOOK FOR ℹ
> Early on in this walk you'll pass a sign for the **Blériot Memorial** and, as it's only a short distance off the main route, it's worth a visit. The memorial commemorates the first successful flight across the English Channel. The *Daily Mail* set a challenge to early aviators offering £1,000 to the first person who could cross the Channel by plane. The prize was won by Frenchman Louis Blériot (1872–1936), who flew from France on 25 July 1909 in a single-engined plane and crash-landed not far from Dover Castle. The flight lasted 37 minutes.

Across the White Cliffs

A loop around St Margaret's at Cliffe.
See map and information panel for Walk 3

•DISTANCE•	2 miles (3.2km)
•MINIMUM TIME•	1hr
•ASCENT / GRADIENT•	328ft (100m) ▲▲▲
•LEVEL OF DIFFICULTY•	🏃🏃 🏃 🏃

Walk 4 Directions (Walk 3 option)

South Foreland Lighthouse dominates the cliffs at Dover. It was built in 1843 to help ships negotiate the treacherous Goodwin Sands that lie offshore. Over the years the Sands have wrecked thousands of vessels – so many that they are known locally as the 'Great Ship Swallower'. At one time, monks used to light fires in caves at the bottom of the cliffs to warn shipping, and in 1635 the first lighthouse was built. The lighthouse you see today earned its place in history on Christmas Eve 1898, when Guglielmo Marconi made the world's first radio transmission to a lightship in the Channel, using his new wireless telegraphy system. His message, relayed in Morse code, read: 'Compliments of the season to all'. A few months later he sent the first international radio message to Wimereux in France.

From Point ⑥ walk round **South Foreland Lighthouse** to meet two tracks. With the lighthouse on your left-hand side, take the metalled track that runs straight ahead. At the end turn right and follow another metalled track, Point Ⓐ.

This takes you past houses with typical seasidey names like Fresh Winds – it gets pretty blowy in the winter here.

At the end of the road turn right, continue to a junction and then take the steep hill on your right. This leads down to the museum at **St Margaret's at Cliffe**, Point Ⓑ. The village was once a rather exclusive resort and the museum celebrates two famous local residents: Ian Fleming (1908–64) and Sir Noël Coward (1899–1973).

From the museum, go through the gate, over the cattle grid and continue ahead. This wide, grassy track offers easy walking and brings you to **South Foreland Lighthouse**. Go left round the lighthouse and rejoin the main walk at Point ⑥ to walk back over the cliffs to Dover.

> **WHILE YOU'RE THERE**
> Not far from St Margaret's at Cliffe is the **Dover Patrol Monument** – one of the many reminders of Dover's historic position in resisting invaders. The Dover Patrol was a fleet of small ships, including trawlers, which kept the Channel open during World War One. The fleet cleared mines dropped by the Germans, and escorted merchant and hospital ships. Over 2,000 men died undertaking this dangerous work.

Walk 5

Birdwatching at Stodmarsh

This easy circuit of a national nature reserve is great for birdwatchers.

•DISTANCE•	4 miles (6.4km)
•MINIMUM TIME•	2hrs 15min
•ASCENT / GRADIENT•	Negligible
•LEVEL OF DIFFICULTY•	
•PATHS•	Wooden walkways, easy footpaths and lanes, 2 stiles
•LANDSCAPE•	Marshlands, meadows and rustling reed beds
•SUGGESTED MAP•	aqua3 OS Explorer 150 Canterbury & the Isle of Thanet
•START / FINISH•	Grid reference: TR 220609
•DOG FRIENDLINESS•	Dogs aren't allowed on nature trail
•PARKING•	Stodmarsh Nature Reserve car park
•PUBLIC TOILETS•	Stodmarsh and Grove Ferry car parks

Walk 5 **Directions**

Bring your binoculars for this walk as it takes you through Stodmarsh National Nature Reserve, one of England's most diverse wetland habitats and a place that simply oozes with bird life. Hidden away in the Stour Valley, the reserve has several types of marshland, shallow lagoons and grazing meadows. There are plenty of hides along the way, from where you can get a closer look. Come in the winter and you'll see wildfowl, while in the spring and autumn there are many migratory birds.

Park at the car park near **Stodmarsh** village. An information board tells you what sort of birds to look out for, including marsh harriers, ruffs, siskins and stonechats. Now follow the signs for the nature trail, which at this point leads you through reed beds, a fast disappearing wildlife habitat. It might look as if this is a natural landscape; in fact it is entirely artificial. Early records show that

monks from a nearby monastery once had a stud farm here (hence the name Stodmarsh – the stud in the marsh). They dug ditches in order to encourage flood water from the Stour on to the surrounding meadows where they grazed their horses.

In the 17th century a flood defence barrier, the Lampen Wall, was built by Flemish refugees, allowing them access to the Wantsum marshes and draining the valley. However, when a coal mine opened here, the underground workings caused subsidence and the land became waterlogged. By the 1930s lagoons had appeared and reed beds began to grow. To preserve this habitat

---

WHILE YOU'RE THERE

Tiny **Fordwich**, near Stodmarsh, was once an important port but is now a pleasantly sleepy village. The church, which dates back to Saxon times, houses the mysterious Fordwich stone, once thought to have formed part of a saint's shrine and a possible hiding place for sacred relics. The village's town hall contains the old village ducking stool.

WHAT TO LOOK FOR ⓘ

Stodmarsh is a tiny village with an equally tiny village green. There's a sundial on it bearing a verse that states cryptically:

> 'Make time, save time
> While time lasts
> All time is no time
> When time is past'.

Make sense of that if you can.

river were once thickly carpeted with lavender bushes that were grown for commercial purposes. The fragrant flowers were cut by hand and then made into lavender water, which was highly sought after by wealthy people. The fields looked spectacular when the plants were in full bloom and people would come from miles around to admire them.

and prevent these sites from reverting to scrub, the water levels in the reserve are controlled and the reed beds are managed by harvesting the reeds and grazing the surrounding meadow.

Cross the bridge over the stream, past benches and over another bridge. At the signpost, follow the nature trail again. The route now takes you over two more bridges and along a wide path to a walkway. You might be lucky and see a bearded tit, a pretty little bird that clings to the stems of reeds and makes a distinctive 'pinging' call. Another bird that loves the reeds is the secretive bittern, a relative of the heron, and one of Britain's most threatened species. Cross another bridge and go through a barrier to another path that takes you along the old **Lampen Wall**. You will soon reach **Lake Tower Hide**, a large hide built on stilts with a great view over the lake.

The path now bears away from the lake and becomes a grassy track. Continue along this, with the **Stour** on your left, until you come to a gate that leads on to the road at **Grove Ferry**. There's a pub here, the **Grove Ferry Inn**, and a pick-up point for boat trips along the river. Turn right and walk down the road, passing signs for a car park and picnic site. The fields bordering the

Carry on down the road and turn right at **Elm Tree Farm**. Walk between the farm and the white cottage, go through a kissing gate and continue past another hide and up to a junction of tracks at another kissing gate. Go left here, then cross a bridge over the stream and carry on until you come to another bridge on your left. Cross this and walk diagonally across the field to cross two more bridges. Go through a gate, turn right, walk down the track, pass through another gate and carry straight on. Nip over the second stile on your right, and then make your way over to another stile and walk ahead on to the track. Your way now takes you past **Undertrees Farm** and down to the road. Turn right along the road back into **Stodmarsh**. If you've got time, stop and have a look at the little church. On one of the doors there are crosses made by Crusaders who stopped off to pray on their way to the coast. Turn right in the village and walk back to the car park.

WHERE TO EAT AND DRINK ⓘ

In Stodmarsh itself, the **Red Lion Inn** offers country cooking and has a garden and a croquet lawn. At Grove Ferry, about half-way round this walk, the **Grove Ferry Inn** serves teas, bar snacks and a good selection of main meals as advertised on a blackboard. In fine weather you can sit outside.

Walk 6

Marching Through Barham

A walk around one of England's most historic areas.

•DISTANCE•	4 miles (6.4km)
•MINIMUM TIME•	2hrs
•ASCENT / GRADIENT•	98ft (30m) ▲ ▲ ▲
•LEVEL OF DIFFICULTY•	🏃 🏃 🏃
•PATHS•	Village streets, tarmac tracks and field margins, 3 stiles
•LANDSCAPE•	Lush downland interspersed with woods
•SUGGESTED MAP•	aqua3 OS Explorer 138 Dover, Folkestone & Hythe
•START / FINISH•	Grid reference: GR 208501
•DOG FRIENDLINESS•	Good, several stretches to run free but keep on lead when near livestock and on golf course
•PARKING•	By Barham green
•PUBLIC TOILETS•	None on route

BACKGROUND TO THE WALK

This walk introduces you to a forgotten corner of Kent. Barham's a pleasant village, but not so picturesque that it makes it on to the standard tourist itinerary; most people have never even heard of it. Yet Barham (pronounced Bar-rum) has witnessed more historic events than many major towns and cities – and they've all had a distinctly military flavour.

A Pageant of History

The village dates from Saxon times and sits snugly by Barham Downs, once described as 'the most historic mile of countryside in England'. It's a title I reckon it deserves. The Roman legions were here first in 54 BC (40,000 of them according to Julius Caesar) camping on the Downs as they battled their way across Kent. The Britons fought hard to repel them, even digging traps that they hid with trees and branches. However, they stood no chance against Caesar's mighty army – particularly after one of their leaders switched sides. Contemporary accounts claim that every single Briton was slain.

During the Norman Conquest of 1066, the Downs were again at the centre of the action, when William the Conqueror met the people of Kent, to hear them swear allegiance to him. He took a few hostages at the same time, just to encourage them to keep their word. Years later King John (1167–1216) camped on Barham Downs with 50,000 men as he prepared to go to war with France, and it was here, too, that Simon de Montfort gathered a huge army during the Barons' War. This began in 1264, after several powerful barons disagreed with the policies of the King, Henry III. Led by Simon de Montfort they took up arms and captured Henry. De Montfort, a French nobleman, then took over control of England, which he ruled until he was killed in 1265.

After that Barham was a peaceful place for a few centuries – until the outbreak of civil war, when Royalist forces assembled here in 1642 before attacking Dover Castle. And then, during the Napoleonic Wars, in the early 19th century, yes, you've guessed it, the army camped on the Downs again before heading off to fight in France. The soldiers seem to have made the most of the opportunites to meet the local women, because the church witnessed plenty of their weddings – and their children were baptised here.

Walk 6

Dad's Army

Barham continued to act as a military magnet in the 20th century. During the First World War the fields were filled with soldiers waiting to go to France and Flanders. And in the Second World War, in an incident reminiscent of an episode of the television series *Dad's Army*, a German aircraft crashed on to the railway line. The crew, who were unharmed, were captured by the local Home Guard.

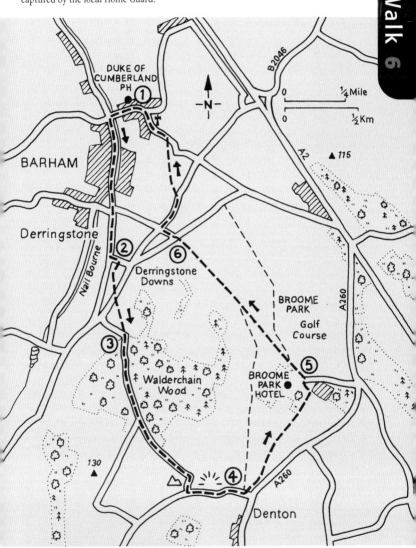

Walk 6 Directions

① From the **Duke of Cumberland** pub by the village green walk down to the main road, then turn left and

walk along **Valley Road** – you'll get great views of the 13th-century church, with its green copper spire, on your left-hand side. Continue up **Derringstone Hill**, then turn left up **Mill Lane**.

Walk 6

② Take the footpath on the right,
go through an area of scrub, cross
over the road, nip over a stile then
go diagonally across the field
heading towards the right-hand
edge of the wood. Continue to
eventually reach a road.

③ Follow the road through the
woods. It's very easy walking here,
and although it's tarmacked you
don't usually meet much traffic.
Pass two houses then go steeply
downhill. At the bottom go left,
signed 'Denton'. The track now
opens out on the right and giving
pleasant views over pasture. Just
before the main road there are two
footpaths leading off to the left;
take the one that forks right.

④ This path eventually leads into
the woods. Pass a house, turn left
and walk down the path, with
tennis courts on the right. Turn
right past the courts and walk
through the grounds of **Broome
Park**. Now a hotel and golf club, the
house was originally built in the
17th century by Inigo Jones for Sir
Basil Dixwell, the man who signed
the, unfulfilled, death warrant of
Charles Edward Stuart (1720–88),
popularly known as Bonnie Prince
Charlie. In the early 20th century it
became the home of Lord Kitchener
of Khartoum (1850–1916), the
celebrated General who gained
notoriety in the First World War. He
featured on the famous poster 'Your
Country Needs You'. Follow the
path through the car park then walk
in front of the house.

⑤ Walk up the track to the first tee,
cross the green (look out for golf
balls) and walk up to the marker
post at the trees. Turn right here,
cross the next green and go over a
stile into the next field. Continue
walking in the direction of **Barham
church**. Cross another field and
come on to the road, through a
kissing gate.

⑥ Cross over to the other side and
walk along the road almost directly
ahead of you. At the crossroads turn
right and head up the road, crossing
a stile on your left to follow a
footpath which brings you up to the
cemetery. Continue to the road at
the church, turn left, follow the
road down and walk back into the
centre of **Barham** village.

A Canterbury Trail

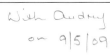

Canterbury's streets have attracted pilgrims for centuries.

•DISTANCE•	3½ miles (5.7km)
•MINIMUM TIME•	1hr 45min
•ASCENT / GRADIENT•	115ft (35m) ▲ ▲ ▲
•LEVEL OF DIFFICULTY•	🚶🚶 🚶🚶 🚶🚶
•PATHS•	City streets and firm footpaths
•LANDSCAPE•	Ancient cathedral city and tracks once followed by pilgrims
•SUGGESTED MAP•	aqua3 OS Explorer 150 Canterbury & the Isle of Thanet
•START / FINISH•	Grid reference: TR 145574
•DOG FRIENDLINESS•	Keep on lead in city but can mostly run free on footpaths
•PARKING•	Castle Street or one of several car parks in Canterbury
•PUBLIC TOILETS•	Castle Row, off Burgate and off High Street

BACKGROUND TO THE WALK

As you walk through the streets of Canterbury, you can't help but be aware that you are following in the footsteps of millions of pilgrims. They have been drawn to Canterbury cathedral every year since 1170, when Thomas Becket was murdered at the cathedral, and have included some notable historic figures. Yet, out of all these people, the most famous pilgrims of all are fictional – they are the characters created by Geoffrey Chaucer (c1345–1400) in his epic poem *The Canterbury Tales* (1387): 'And specially from every shires ende, Of Engelond to Caunterbury they wende'.

Roving Ambassador

Chaucer is acknowledged as the father of English literature, but writing wasn't his main occupation, in fact it was just a hobby. His life was so varied it reads a bit like a work of fiction itself. Chaucer was born while the Hundred Years War was raging between England and France, and after several years working in the Royal household, he joined the army. He was taken prisoner in France but was eventually released after the English paid a ransom for him. That would probably have been enough excitement for anyone in their lifetime, but instead of sinking into domesticity Chaucer then became a sort of roving ambassador travelling throughout Europe on various high level diplomatic missions. He could read French, Latin and Italian and when he travelled he took the opportunity to study foreign literature, which he put to good use in his own works. Back in England, he took on various official posts including customs controller of furs, skins and hides, and knight of the shire for Kent. He also found time to write several long poems and translate many works of prose.

He wrote *The Canterbury Tales* around 1387 and created a cast of lively, believable characters that tell us a great deal about life in the 14th century. There's the earthy Wife of Bath, who's already had five husbands and seems to have set out on this pilgrimage to catch her sixth; the too worldly Prioress, who puts on affected table manners and speaks French – unfortunately more like Del Boy Trotter than anything else; and then there's the corrupt Friar, who's not at all bothered about those in need, but who sells absolution to anyone who can afford it. The poem, written in Middle English, became the first printed work of English literature and is known all over the world. Chaucer is buried in Westminster Abbey.

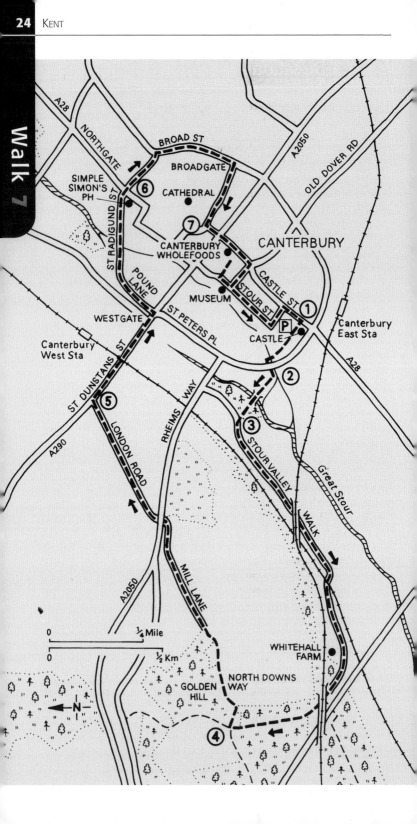

Walk 7

Walk 7 Directions

① Go right from **Castle Street** car park then right again past the castle. At the end turn left on **Centenary Walk**. Where this finishes go right and walk beside the road. Cross a bridge, turn left, go under another bridge and along the river to the other side of the road.

② Cross some grassland, go over a bridge and through a children's play area. Walk across the car park and turn left up the road to join the **Stour Valley Walk**.

③ Go under a bridge and continue to a level crossing. Cross the railway, then stroll up past **Whitehall Farm**. Walk under the arch, through a gate and over a stream. The path bends round and the main road is on your left. At a junction turn right along the **North Downs Way**.

④ Go over a bridge and up a lane. To your left is **Golden Hill** – the point from which pilgrims traditionally had their first view of the city. When you come to a track, turn left and follow it round. Go right along **Mill Lane** to the main road. Take the underpass to cross **Rheims Way**, walk down **London Road**, then turn right into **St Dunstans Street**.

⑤ Walk down into Canterbury to the **Westgate**, turn left along **Pound Lane** and into **St Radigund Street**, with **Simple Simon's** pub on the right-hand side.

⑥ Continue into **Northgate**, go left then right down **Broad Street**. You're now walking around the outside of the city walls. Turn right along Burgate, past a tiny 16th-century building called the Pilgrim's Shop. Soon come to a pedestrianised area that brings you out at the **Butter Market** and war memorial. On your right-hand side is the entrance to the cathedral.

⑦ Turn left and walk down the road, pass the tourist information centre and then turn right to **Stour Street**. On the right is the city museum, set in the ancient **Poor Priests' Hospital** and almost opposite, down **Jewry Lane**, is Canterbury Wholefoods where you can finish your walk with tea and cakes. To return to **Castle Street**, turn left on **Rosemary Lane** and then right.

WHERE TO EAT AND DRINK
Two places are well worth investigating. **Canterbury Wholefoods** on Jewry Lane has a café upstairs, with organic cakes and snacks. **Simple Simon's** on St Radigund Street is a friendly pub in a medieval building. Here you'll find baked potatoes, sandwiches and real ales.

WHAT TO LOOK FOR ⓘ
Canterbury Cathedral was the first cathedral built in England. It was founded in AD 597 by St Augustine. The present structure dates back to 1071 and is a spectacular example of ecclesiastical architecture. However, it was a murder that first attracted pilgrims to the cathedral. In 1170 Thomas Becket, the Archbishop of Canterbury, was killed by men loyal to the King, Henry II. The Primate had only just returned from exile, after a disagreement with Henry over constitutional reform. The King was overcome with guilt, following the murder, and made a pilgrimage to the cathedral, walking barefoot to show his humility. Becket was buried at Canterbury and was credited with so many miracles that he was soon canonised. The city was established as a site of pilgrimage.

Walk 8

The Heart of Bishopsbourne

Discover the country home of author Joseph Conrad and a peculiar coincidence involving James Bond.

•DISTANCE•	4 miles (6.4km)
•MINIMUM TIME•	2hrs
•ASCENT / GRADIENT•	328ft (100m) ▲▲▲
•LEVEL OF DIFFICULTY•	👫 👫 👫
•PATHS•	Narrow lanes and field paths
•LANDSCAPE•	Country house parkland, agricultural fields and orchards
•SUGGESTED MAP•	aqua3 OS Explorer 150 Canterbury & the Isle of Thanet
•START / FINISH•	Grid reference: TR 188526
•DOG FRIENDLINESS•	Good, can mostly run free except around Bourne House
•PARKING•	On street in Bishopsbourne, especially near Mermaid Inn
•PUBLIC TOILETS•	None on route

BACKGROUND TO THE WALK

Get your boots on, synchronise your watches and pack your satellite locator – you probably won't need them, but this walk is filled with reminders of a couple of all action heroes; a swashbuckling sailor and a fictional spy.

A Seafaring Smuggler

Polish writer Joseph Conrad (1857–1924) came to Bishopsbourne in 1919. He was the author of many novels, but could hardly have invented a more entertaining story than that of his own life. Born Jósef Teodor Konrad Nalecz Korzeniowski in 1857 in Berdichev, Poland (now in the Ukraine), Conrad lost both his parents at an early age. He left Poland as soon as he could and went to Marseilles to join the French merchant navy.

Conrad travelled widely and was involved with the smuggling trade, running guns to supporters of Don Carlos VII, who was trying (unsuccessfully as it turned out) to claim the Spanish throne. As with all good stories, Conrad fell in love with one of Carlos' supporters, a Basque woman named Dona Rita. The relationship must have been stormy and passionate, for he fought a duel over her, his opponent was an American called Captain Blunt. Neither man died, but both were wounded – Conrad narrowly missed being shot through the heart. It didn't do him much good for his Spanish lover went off with Captain Blunt anyway.

Heart of Darkness

Shortly before he was 21 Conrad took a job on a British ship. He learned English, passed his captain's exams and in 1884 became a naturalised British subject. He travelled to wild and remote places, such as Borneo, Singapore and Australia. He also went up river in the Belgian Congo, a part of Africa known as the 'white man's graveyard'. This inspired his novel *Heart of Darkness* (which in turn, inspired Francis Ford Coppola's Vietnam epic *Apocalypse Now*), but also seriously undermined his health.

Walk 8

The Quiet Life

Eventually Conrad gave up his rather wild seafaring ways and settled down quietly in Kent. He took to writing, simplifying his name as he guessed – correctly – that no one would be able to get their tongue round Korzeniowski. He spent the last five years of his life at Bishopsbourne, living at Oswalds, a little house by the church.

One of Conrad's novels was entitled *The Secret Agent* (1907) and he probably would have made a great James Bond. By coincidence, one of the James Bond books, *You Only Live Twice* (1964) was written at the Duck pub at nearby Pett Bottom. Ian Fleming, who wrote the books, lived in Kent, when he wasn't living in Jamaica, and frequently took his inspiration from the area. In fact James Bond's code name was taken from the number 007 bus that ran by Fleming's home near Dover. I don't know whether the Duck ever served martinis – shaken, not stirred – but if he'd been around Joseph Conrad would no doubt have tried one.

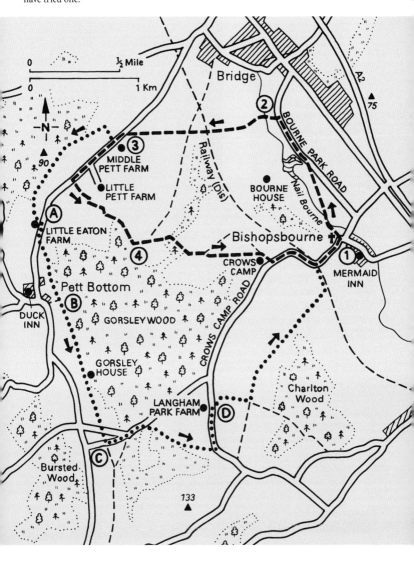

Walk 8 Directions

① From the church, walk through the graveyard following the **Elham Valley Way**. While you're here, have a look for the grave of the Revd Joseph Bancroft Reade. A former rector of the church, he was an enlightened chap and one of only a handful of religious men who felt that Darwin's theory of evolution did not go against the teachings of the Bible. At a waymarker, bear right across pasture for about 200yds (183m) then cross a bridge over the Nail Bourne. Nip over another stile and continue through the parkland of **Bourne House**, passing the lake on your left. After 650yds (594m) cross a stile and turn left into **Bourne Park Road**. Stroll past the gates of Bourne House and continue until you reach two cottages on the right.

② Turn left down the lane and cross the stream again. Follow the lane until it peters out near a farm and hop gardens, then continue ahead between the hedges. There's a gentle climb now, across a bridge and up to the top of the hill. Cross a stile at the right-hand corner of the field, then descend into the valley walking diagonally over the fields towards the distant high hedge (use the pylon on the horizon as a marker). Now nip over the stile, turn right round the orchard

margin and after about 300yds (274m) cut over another stile on your right. Turn left and walk along the road to **Middle Pett Farm**.

③ Continue walking ahead, pass **Little Pett Farm** and then turn left to head up the footpath. Cross a stile at the top left-hand corner of a field and follow the signs round the left-hand margin of the next field, turning right at the cattle trough. Continue to cross a stile on the left, then walk left around the next field and continue uphill towards the corner of the woodland. Follow the left-hand side of the wood and, after about 400yds (366m), turn sharp left, away from the wood and cross the field to the marker post by the holly hedge.

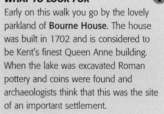

WHAT TO LOOK FOR

Early on this walk you go by the lovely parkland of **Bourne House**. The house was built in 1702 and is considered to be Kent's finest Queen Anne building. When the lake was excavated Roman pottery and coins were found and archaeologists think that this was the site of an important settlement.

④ Fork right across the field, turn right into the woodland and follow the track. Emerge into open fields and soon go sharp left. Fork right at the first telegraph pole and walk across a large field heading towards the chimneys of **Crows Camp** ahead. Pass to the left of the garden hedge, turn left at the road and walk back into **Bishopsbourne**.

WHERE TO EAT AND DRINK

The **Mermaid Inn** at Bishopsbourne is a CAMRA (Campaign for Real Ale) recommended pub and serves excellent lunches. You can also stop off on your walk to visit the **Duck Inn** at Pett Bottom, which serves good food. The nearby village of Bridge has several pubs and a good bakery.

WHILE YOU'RE THERE

Bishopsbourne church dates back to the 13th century. It has medieval floor tiles, stained glass and wall paintings. Take a look at the west window by the Arts and Crafts artists Edward Burne-Jones and William Morris.

And Past Pett Bottom

A longer walk past a pub that has associations with 007.
See map and information panel for Walk 8

•DISTANCE•	6 miles (9.7km)
•MINIMUM TIME•	2hrs 45min
•ASCENT / GRADIENT•	482ft (147m) ▲▲▲
•LEVEL OF DIFFICULTY•	🚶🚶 🚶🚶 🚶

Walk 9 Directions (Walk 8 option)

From Point ③ turn right opposite the entrance to **Middle Pett Farm** and follow the byway. Turn left at a waymarked post, walk between orchards and, at a post in the centre of the path, continue ahead along the margin of the wood. Keep to this path as it descends and you'll eventually pass through a gate into pasture, where you walk towards a strip of woodland ahead. At the left-hand corner of the hedge, climb the metal gate and descend to **Little Eaton Farm**, walking between a wire fence and a high hedge. Rejoin **Pett Bottom Road** at a thatched barn.

Turn right on to the road, Point Ⓐ, and continue until you reach a stile on your left. Nip over this and then climb diagonally through the fields to the corner of **Gorsley Wood**. Pop through a hole in the fence (it's just past the pylon) and follow the narrow path that skirts along the side of the wood. Soon reach another track that leads down to the **Duck Inn**, Point Ⓑ.

Unless you're desperate for a drink, continue on the main track until you reach a large concrete building. Cross a stile here and follow the footpath until you cross another stile at the gates of **Gorsley House**. Your route now continues ahead, over two more stiles and through open pastureland until you reach a tarmac lane. Turn left here, Point Ⓒ, walk through the wood then, where the lane bears left, take the byway that runs ahead into a small wood.

After an iron gate, the track now descends gradually to **Pheasants Hall Lane**, where you turn left and walk down to **Langham Park Farm**, Point Ⓓ. There's a lovely old Kentish barn here, with low eaves and a steeply pitched roof. Take the bridleway up through the trees to the right. Fork right at the top into open fields, follow the track until you reach a path on the left and walk towards the wood. Bear slightly to the right after this and head across the field towards a high wooded hedge, using a dead tree as a marker. Pass through this hedge and continue in the same direction for about ½ mile (800m). Turn left at the junction of farm tracks and make your way downhill to join **Crows Camp Road**. Turn right here, go over the old iron railway bridge and make your way back to **Bishopsbourne**.

Walk 10

Blean's Ancient Woodlands

A chance to enjoy one of England's oldest woods.

•DISTANCE•	5 miles (8km)
•MINIMUM TIME•	2hrs 45min
•ASCENT / GRADIENT•	82ft (50m) ▲ ▲ ▲
•LEVEL OF DIFFICULTY•	🚶🚶 🚶 🚶
•PATHS•	Field and woodland paths, poorly waymarked in places, 11 stiles
•LANDSCAPE•	Farmland and tracts of ancient forest
•SUGGESTED MAP•	aqua3 OS Explorer 150 Canterbury & the Isle of Thanet
•START / FINISH•	Grid reference: TR 136629
•DOG FRIENDLINESS•	Can run free except close to A290 and grazing animals
•PARKING•	Woodland car park at Gypsy Corner
•PUBLIC TOILETS•	None on route

Walk 10 Directions

The ancient forest of Blean once stretched across a vast expanse of countryside to the north of Canterbury. Patches of this woodland still exist, and there are plenty of paths that lead through them. This is just one walk you can follow and it gives you a great chance to observe a wide range of wildlife. Ancient woodland is that which can be traced back to around 1600, when the earliest maps were produced, and contains native trees such as birch, oak, hornbeam and hazel. A good way of identifying an ancient wood is by the presence of certain wild flowers, called indicator species. These plants don't spread easily and aren't found in great numbers in more modern woodlands. They include bluebells, anemones, wild garlic, dogs mercury, woodland orchids, butcher's broom and herb paris.

Start at the **Clowes Wood** car park at **Gypsy Corner**. Walk back along **Hackington Road** for about for about ¼ mile (400m). Do take care as it's a busy road and there is no footpath. Take the second path on the right – a public bridleway. Pass through some woodland and then go on, beside arable fields and under pylons, to **Well Court**. As you approach the farm, turn left at the poly tunnels and then turn right at the static caravan. Continue to follow the track through the farm, past a willow tree and on past new greenhouses on your right. Your way now takes you between arable fields, through a high hedge and on to a junction of paths. Turn left here between high hedges.

Your path eventually joins a metalled cycle track. Follow the smartly fenced paddock on the left, round to the road. Cross **Tyler Hill Road** and make your way round right and left to pass Blean church. The graveyard here is said to contain the unmarked grave of a young child called Agnes Gibbs. She never grew properly and her tiny body became something of a local curiosity. Queen Victoria's mother heard about her and had the little girl sent to London so she could see her for herself. Agnes was even examined by the Queen's doctor. Sadly she didn't live long and died at the age of two – only 18 inches (46cm) tall. Medical science was still in its infancy, and her father feared that her body might be dug up by grave robbers who often supplied surgeons with bodies to dissect, so, with the help of the vicar, he buried Agnes at night in an unmarked grave.

> **WHERE TO EAT AND DRINK** ⓘ
> The **Hare and Hounds** on the A290 serves breakfasts as well as main meals, snacks and hot drinks. There are also several pubs in Blean.

Continue on the cycle track to a bridge across a stream. Turn right here into a field and follow the trees beside the stream to the corner of the field. Cross the stile and the wooden footbridge. Continue through woodland with the stream on your left. The path soon veers right and slightly uphill into a paddock. Go left through a kissing gate and on into the car park of the **Hare and Hounds** pub on the **A290**. Cross the main road and turn left over the stream, then right where a metal farm gate is set back from the road. Pass through the white gate and then follow the path round the woodland to the left. After 300yds (274m), at the end of the open paddock, turn right and,

with the high hedge to your left, walk down to the corner. Cross a small wooden bridge, nip over a stile and through a small paddock.

Cross another stream and go along the edge of a field, crossing three more stiles before you come on to a concrete farm road. Turn right and immediately go through the wrought iron gates to follow the road back to the **A290**. Cross the road and turn left up the footpath, pass **Tyler Hill Road** and eventually turn right into **Chapel Lane**. Go left immediately after the converted chapel. The narrow path passes between gardens, then goes left at **Badgers' Farm House** into a field. At the end of the field turn right on to a concrete lane, then continue through the gate marked **Butler's Court Farm**. When you come to two stiles, cross the one on the right-hand side eventually to go over a stiled footbridge.

Cross the field ahead, pass to the right of the cottage garden, go over a stile and left into the tarmac lane. Walk along the lane, then fork left opposite **Arbele Farm** into the field. Your way now takes you across two fields and two stiles, before you turn left, back into the lane. Where the lane forks continue on the narrow path between high hedges and towards **Clowes Wood**. The path continues into the wood, with low branches overhead. At a crossing of tracks continue ahead and walk back to the car park.

> **WHAT TO LOOK FOR** ⓘ
> If you explore Blean Woods keep your eyes peeled for **herb paris**, often found under beech trees and an indicator of ancient woodland. It's an unusual plant, the four leaves near the top of the stem are arranged just below the single, green star-shaped flower. It was once believed to have magical properties and although the berries are poisonous, they were eaten as protection against witchcraft or the plague (don't try this at home). For some reason, tradition dictated that an odd number of berries should be eaten.

The Holy Maid of Aldington

There are memories of a forgotten visionary and a notorious gang of smugglers on this walk.

•DISTANCE•	3 miles (4.8km)
•MINIMUM TIME•	2hrs 30min
•ASCENT / GRADIENT•	66ft (20m)
•LEVEL OF DIFFICULTY•	
•PATHS•	Waymarked tracks and badly signposted field paths, 8 stiles
•LANDSCAPE•	Rolling pasture and fields and site of a former Archbishop's Palace
•SUGGESTED MAP•	aqua3 OS Explorer 137 Ashford
•START / FINISH•	Grid reference: TQ 064355
•DOG FRIENDLINESS•	Keep on lead
•PARKING•	On street in Aldington
•PUBLIC TOILETS•	None on route

BACKGROUND TO THE WALK

It's never been easy being a visionary – as one woman from Aldington found to her cost. Her name was Elizabeth Barton and she was born in 1506, a time when superstition, politics and religion were closely intertwined. When Elizabeth was young she was taken on as a servant in the household of Thomas Cobb, the Archbishop of Canterbury's local steward who looked after the Archbishops' Palace that once stood here.

A Tudor Mystic Meg

In 1525 Elizabeth began to suffer from fits and would go into deep trances. When she came round she would tell people about events that were happening some way off, or would mention strange images she had seen. Her parish priest soon came to believe that she was having divine visions – although historians today think they were probably epileptic fits. With the priest's encouragement, Elizabeth began to make her 'prophecies' more widely known and hundreds of pilgrims were soon flocking to see her at Aldington.

Elizabeth was credited with some minor miracles and William Warham, the Archbishop of Canterbury, became interested in her visions. She was eventually allotted a religious cell at a convent in Canterbury and became known as the Holy Maid of Kent. Unfortunately for her, the Church was in turmoil at the time, for Henry VIII was planning to divorce his wife, Catherine of Aragon, and marry Anne Boleyn. The authorities realised that Elizabeth's visions gave them the ideal opportunity to prevent the marriage, and so stop England breaking away from the Catholic Church in Rome. Elizabeth was poor and uneducated and they could see that she would be easy to manipulate. They cleverly encouraged her to prophesy that if the marriage to Anne went ahead, Henry would lose his kingdom – not the most tactful of things to say given Henry's extremely ruthless nature.

A Date at Tyburn

The Archbishop of Canterbury, who had supported Elizabeth, was arrested and his successor, Thomas Cranmer, set up a commission to investigate her prophesies. The inquiry took months and in the end Elizabeth was forced to confess – no doubt aided by a bit of gentle torture – that she had never had visions at all. Along with several of the monks who had installed her at Canterbury, she was tried for treason and in April 1534, they were all executed at Tyburn in London. Elizabeth was aged just 28. Today, few people have heard of Kent's unfortunate oracle and the Archbishops' Palace has crumbled away. You walk past what remains of it at Court Lodge Farm, near the rather lonely church.

In later years, Aldington gained further notoriety as the headquarters of the Aldington Gang of smugglers, probably formed by soldiers returning from the Napoleonic Wars. They operated from the Walnut Tree Inn at Aldington Corner, where this walk starts.

Walk 11

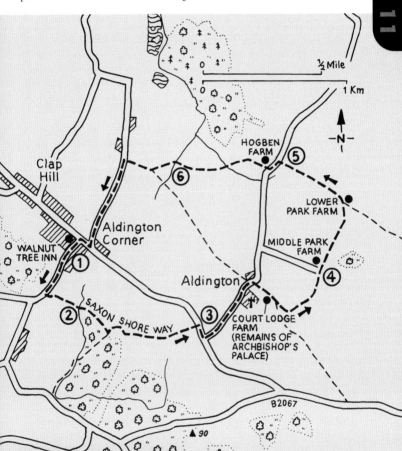

Walk 11 Directions

① From the **Walnut Tree Inn** at Aldington Corner, walk up **Forge Road**. At a path on the left cross a stile to join the **Saxon Shore Way**. Walk across the field, hop over another stile, turn left and follow a waymarker downhill. Cross a stile into the woods.

② Walk through the woods, nip over a stile and, still on the **Saxon Shore Way**, follow the fence line, then bear left and come up through pasture. Go through a rusty gate and come on to the road.

Walk 11

③ Turn right and continue ahead, then go left up the road, past **Aldington church**. Take the track that leads to the right past some cottages. This was once the site of an archbishop's palace. Henry VIII rather liked it so took it for himself during the Reformation. There's nothing to be seen of it today. Continue to a wooden gate, go along the vehicle track, then follow the treeline down to a stile. Follow the fence line on the right, cross a stile and continue down to **Middle Park Farm**.

④ Walk through the farm where you might see some peacocks strutting about. Cross the metal gate into the field and continue ahead with the hedgerow on your left, walking under pylons. Continue walking along the fenceline and then take the track round the front of **Lower Park Farm**, over the overgrown stile. Come on to a shingle track and bear slightly left with hedgerows on your right. Go over the cattle grid and come on to the road.

⑤ Turn left down the road, then turn right on to the drive of **Hogben Farm**. Walk down the drive, then go left through the wooden gate into the paddock. Climb over the wooden gate ahead, then walk straight across the field,

---

WHILE YOU'RE THERE ⓘ

If you've got children with you, promise them a visit to the **South of England Rare Breeds Centre** at Woodchurch, a short drive from Aldington. Set in extensive grounds there are lots of traditional breeds of farm animals, including all seven of Britain's rare pigs. There are also cattle, horses, goats, poultry and rabbits.

---

heading to the bottom left-hand corner. Go through a gap in the hedgerow and cross the field under the pylons.

⑥ Cross a stream, then go diagonally across the field to a lone tree in the corner. Climb a stile then cut diagonally across the field to the top left-hand corner. After going through another gap in the hedge you climb another stile. Now go diagonally right across the field and head down to the main road. Go left then walk down the main road and back into the village.

WHAT TO LOOK FOR ⓘ

Aldington has literary associations too. Noël Coward (1899–1973) lived here for many years and wrote some of his most famous songs in the village. *A Room with a View* (1928), by E M Foster, was said to have been inspired by the view from his window. The author Ford Madox Ford also lived locally, in a house called Aldington Knoll which overlooked Romney Marsh.

WHERE TO EAT AND DRINK ⓘ

The **Walnut Tree Inn** at Aldington Corner is owned by Shepherd Neame, Britain's oldest brewer. The usual bar snacks like jacket potatoes, baguettes and sandwiches are available along with an excellent choice of pies such as steak, mushroom and Guinness, or salmon and broccoli, and Sunday roasts. Food is available for lunch and dinner, except on Monday evenings.

A Crafty Walk Through Perry Wood

This circular route takes you through working woodland.

•DISTANCE•	4 miles (6.4km)
•MINIMUM TIME•	2hrs
•ASCENT / GRADIENT•	345ft (105m) ▲▲▲
•LEVEL OF DIFFICULTY•	🚶🚶 🚶🚶 🚶
•PATHS•	Woodland paths and field margins, 7 stiles
•LANDSCAPE•	Working woodland, orchards and fields
•SUGGESTED MAP•	aqua3 OS Explorer 149 Sittingbourne & Faversham
•START / FINISH•	Grid reference: TQ 045556
•DOG FRIENDLINESS•	Can mostly run free, except in orchards and pasture
•PARKING•	Woodland car park in Perry Wood
•PUBLIC TOILETS•	None on route

BACKGROUND TO THE WALK

Traditional country crafts seem to have practically died out in Britain, but on this walk through Perry Wood you'll see that one, at least, is still being practised. It's the craft of coppicing and you'll see evidence of it early in this walk.

A Multitude of Uses

Coppicing, which comes from the French word 'couper' to cut, is an ancient way of managing woodland. When small trees are cut down they soon send up new shoots from the base. If there is plenty of light around them they grow tall and straight – providing a useful supply of timber that can be used for a wide range of purposes: it can be made into charcoal and firewood, woven into hurdles, cut into pea sticks, used to make hop poles, or turned into sturdy fence posts. Different woods have different qualities. Ash, for example, absorbs shock well, so is very good for making tool handles.

The most commonly coppiced wood today is sweet chestnut, which is highly durable and weathers to a dark grey. It is used to make fence posts, palings and hop poles. The species was introduced to Britain by the Romans, probably to provide a ready supply of chestnut flour for the legionaries, who longed for food like mama made. When blocks (or 'coups') of trees are coppiced they can go on producing wood for hundreds of years. Sweet chestnut grows very quickly and can be harvested every 12–15 years.

Flourishing Wildlife

The beauty of coppicing is not simply that it provides timber without destroying trees. It also helps to provide a valuable habitat for wildlife. That might sound strange but it works like this: whenever the trees are coppiced, a clear patch is created in the wood. As the sun floods in, wild flowers like bluebells, sage and foxgloves spring up. You'll also see willow herb, often known as fireweed because it loves to grow on ground that has been disturbed. These plants in turn attract insects such as butterflies and beetles. In time the trees begin to grow back, creating a scrubby area that is an ideal breeding ground for birds.

In chestnut coppice you find an extraordinary range of bird species, including blackcaps, chiffchaffs, yellowhammers and nightingales. Eventually the chestnut coppice grows tall and creates a dense canopy. This is not quite as attractive to wildlife, so they move on to the next cleared area. The seeds of the plants remain dormant in the soil then spring into life when the plot is cleared again. As well as sweet chestnut, you'll see oaks, beeches and Scots pine as you wander through this working woodland.

Walk 12 Directions

① From the woodland car park, cross the road and plunge into the wood, walking south along the bridleway. You'll soon see evidence of recent coppicing. After a few hundred paces skirt to the left and cross the boggy ground over the boardwalk. Cross the track at **Keeper's Cottage** gateway and bear

Walk 12

left then right. Climb through the woods, bear left at the top and out into open heathland (I know, it looks like woodland on the OS map). Walk along the ridge and climb to the observation platform for some great views over the surrounding countryside.

② Walk past the picnic area then enter an orchard by a stile. Continue ahead towards the bungalow at the top of the orchard. Skirt left around the garden and drop down on to the tarmac lane by a stile.

③ Turn right to reach the centre of **Shottenden**, continue straight on at the junction, pass the white weatherboarded cottage and continue up to the crossroads.

④ Turn left into **Denne Manor Lane**, walk past a disused oast house and continue between fields. Fork right under a line of pylons and continue across arable fields towards a telegraph pole. Maintain

direction to walk through a small gate and continue past fields. Your path eventually joins a rough farm track, and then bears left to a tarmac lane at **Wytherling Court**.

⑤ Turn right and right again at the next two T-junctions. Soon come to a house and turn left to walk along a wiggly lane. Turn right at the main road and then join a footpath on the left.

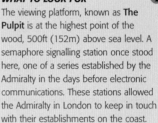

⑥ Your way now lies ahead across open fields. Aim for the lone oak tree on the skyline, and walk down through the first field, crossing the barbed wire fence by a broken stile. Continue over the next field and sheep pasture, climbing three more stiles to join the lane.

⑦ Turn right into the tarmac lane, where your path soon dives left across fields again, towards a Georgian house. At the lane, cross to go over another field and back into the wood by a stile.

⑧ Follow the path to the left and continue to cross the lane and go through a paddock. Leave this at the bottom corner, then scramble through an overgrown area into the wood, and then go through a garden and on to the lane. Turn right, return through the wood and then go left at the crossroads and back to the car park.

Mr Darcy's Chilham

A lovely walk in countryside strongly associated with Jane Austen.

•DISTANCE•	5 miles (8km)
•MINIMUM TIME•	2hrs 30min
•ASCENT / GRADIENT•	131ft (40m) ▲▲▲
•LEVEL OF DIFFICULTY•	🚶 🚶 🚶
•PATHS•	Parkland, field paths and woodland tracks, 8 stiles
•LANDSCAPE•	Rolling Kentish countryside with views of Chilham Castle
•SUGGESTED MAP•	aqua3 OS Explorer 149 Sittingbourne & Faversham
•START / FINISH•	Grid reference: TQ 068536
•DOG FRIENDLINESS•	Good, though must be kept on lead near grazing animals
•PARKING•	Chilham car park
•PUBLIC TOILETS•	Chilham

BACKGROUND TO THE WALK

Imagine you're a young, single woman staying with your brother at his elegant country mansion. One morning you walk to Chilham, a pretty village near by. Across the fields you spot a dark haired man in tight breeches, cantering towards you on a glossy chestnut horse. As he nears you, he slows down and says, 'Good Morning', and you feel his eyes bore deep into your own. Your heart does a somersault. The man rides off. That night in bed you think about your hero and christen him – Mr Darcy. Well, it could have happened, for this walk takes you through the idyllic countryside that inspired Jane Austen. And her most famous novel, *Pride and Prejudice* (originally entitled *First Impressions*) was written here in 1796.

Brother Edward

Although Jane Austen is more usually associated with Hampshire, she spent a great deal of time in Kent visiting her brother Edward, who had a rather unusual upbringing. Jane came from a large family and had six brothers and a sister. When Edward was young he stayed with some wealthy relatives, the Knights, who were unable to have children of their own. Edward was adopted by the Knights and went to live at Godmersham House, a handsome, red brick mansion set in rolling parkland, which you pass on this walk. The Knights doted on Edward, they educated him and sent him on the Grand Tour. When Mr Knight died, Edward inherited Godmersham, changing his surname to Knight.

Jane frequently stayed at Godmersham House, she dined at Chilham Castle, called on local families, worshipped in Godmersham church, and walked in the countryside. She led a sheltered life and the characters in her novels were drawn from the people she met at society balls and concerts. Jane didn't always enjoy these events and particularly hated the social life of Bath, where she complained about attending 'another stupid party'. She was a skilled observer of people and once said that all she needed for a novel were three or four families in a village. She almost certainly wrote about people she met at Chilham. Godmersham House featured in her books. There's a small door in the wall around the park that was used by the Revd Collins in *Pride and Prejudice*, and the house and grounds were probably the model for *Mansfield Park*. Jane Austen died in 1817, aged only 41, but she captured forever the lives of the society people who once lived in this idyllic corner of Kent.

Walk 13

Walk 13 Directions

① From the village square, walk down **School Lane** and follow the road past **Chilham Castle** and up to **April Cottage**. Here you take the footpath on the left – there's a waymarker on the telegraph pole.

② You now pass between the gardens, then fork right across the field to the hedge in the far corner. Nip over the stile and into the water-meadows beside the **Great Stour**. Follow the hedge and continue until you come to a bridge. Your path bears right here, then takes you over a narrow footbridge on to the busy **A28**. Turn left here, walk up to **East Stour Farm**, then turn right and walk through the farmyard, cross a stile and go under the railway bridge.

③ Follow the path ahead that bears to the left and rises up the valley. Keep an eye out for badger setts in the hedge along here. Continue ahead and follow the **Stour Valley Walk** as it bears right.

④ At a crossing of paths, continue along the Stour Valley Walk, go through the wood, and then cross a stile. Continue up a field and into more woodland, where you soon

turn right to follow the **Stour Valley Walk**. Descend to the road crossing two more stiles – look back for great views of **Chilham Castle**.

⑤ Walk to **Woodsdale Farm** and hop over the stile opposite. Walk diagonally uphill to the top corner (there are ivy-covered trees on the skyline), cross another stile and then walk a short distance ahead before forking right along the **Stour Valley Walk**. Follow this as it takes you diagonally down the fields towards a pair of trees in the hedge. Continue in the same direction and cross a stile on to **Eggarton Lane**.

> **WHERE TO EAT AND DRINK**
> You can get good light meals at the **Copper Kettle** tea room in Chilham, while the **White Horse** pub does bar food and Sunday lunches.

⑥ Turn right, walk down the lane, and then turn right again under the railway and up to the **A28**. Cross over and walk along the lane ahead. After crossing the Great Stour, go through the gates of the College of Education and right into the parkland of **Godmersham Park**.

⑦ Follow the public footpath through the paddocks and up past the house. At the top corner, take the footpath to the right and walk ahead, through a gate and on to the road. Follow this road all the way back into **Chilham**.

> **WHAT TO LOOK FOR**
> **Chilham Castle** is not open to the public, but you do get some good views of it on this walk. A castle was built here after the Norman Conquest, but the main house on the estate today is a Jacobean mansion, probably designed by Inigo Jones. The parkland has the oldest heronry in the country. It is said that if the herons don't return to nest here by St Valentine's Day, then terrible things will happen to the owner of the castle.

> **WHILE YOU'RE THERE**
> During the Second World War, **Godmersham Park** was the site of an underground hide-out for Kent's secret guerrilla army. This had been formed by Peter Fleming, a captain in the Grenadier Guards and the brother of Ian Fleming, creator of James Bond, to offer resistance if Kent was ever invaded.

And Past Chilham's Ancient Burial Ground

A longer walk taking in a mysterious burial site.
See map and information panel for Walk 13

•DISTANCE•	7½ miles (12.1km)
•MINIMUM TIME•	4hrs
•ASCENT / GRADIENT•	443ft (135m) ▲▲▲
•LEVEL OF DIFFICULTY•	🚶 🚶 🚶

Walk 14 Directions (Walk 13 option)

From the village square, Point ①, go to the church and walk to the left-hand corner of the churchyard. Head down to the tarmac lane and continue to cross the A252. Go over the crossroads and up **Long Hill**. Shortly after **Cork Farm**, turn right on to a narrow footpath. At the tarmac road, cross and follow the path ahead. This soon brings you on to a narrow lane, Point Ⓐ, where you turn right, then left beside the orchard – there's a house called **Plumtrees** on the right. Pass a concrete barn and walk past orchards to a metal gate. Go through this, then follow the track to **Bowerland Farm**, Point Ⓑ.

Cross the stile, go through the farmyard (it can get pretty muddy) and continue to **Bowerland Lane**. Walk down the lane to the **A28** and cross to the footpath opposite. Turn right, walk beside the road for a short distance, then go left on to a narrow footpath. Soon cross a stile and go through a garden. The route now takes you across the railway line, Point Ⓒ, and into **Pickelden**

Lane. Follow the lane until it bends sharply left, where you cross a stile and turn right, Point Ⓓ.

Go through a field, nip over a couple of stiles and eventually enter a back garden. Drop into the lane over another stile to **Stile Farm**. Go to the right in front of the cottage, then left into the fields. Skirt round the edge of the first field keeping the hedge on your right, then join a track that leads past the Great Stour. Reach a track that leads left, up the side of the valley, Point Ⓔ. Walk uphill, over a stile and into the fields. Cross a stile at a waymarker and turn right on to a track – you're now on the **Stour Valley Walk**.

Near this spot is Julliberrie Long Barrow, a neolithic burial site that was later re-used to bury a Romano-British family. For many years it was thought to contain the body of Julius Laverius, one of Caesar's officers who was killed here in an early skirmish with the British. In fact his grave has never been found – you never know, it could be near by, just a few feet from your path. Continue walking ahead, over a path junction, until you cross a stile, turn left and join the main walk at Point ③.

Across Romney Marshes

An atmospheric walk across moody marshlands.

•DISTANCE•	3 miles (4.8km)
•MINIMUM TIME•	1hr 30min
•ASCENT / GRADIENT•	Negligible
•LEVEL OF DIFFICULTY•	
•PATHS•	Field edges, lanes and some road, can be muddy
•LANDSCAPE•	Moody marshlands
•SUGGESTED MAP•	aqua3 OS Explorer 125 Romney Marsh, Rye & Winchelsea
•START / FINISH•	Grid reference: TR 028277
•DOG FRIENDLINESS•	Must be kept on a lead by roads due to speeding traffic
•PARKING•	Near Bell Inn at Ivychurch
•PUBLIC TOILETS•	None on route

Walk 15 Directions

In *The Ingoldsby Legends* (1837) Revd Richard Barham declared that the world: 'is divided into Europe, Asia, Africa, America and Romney Marsh'. You'll certainly find it hard to believe that you're in Kent. The flat, windy marshlands, topped with enormous sweeping skies, present an unusual picture in southern England. Stretching endlessly to the horizon, the marshes are laced with watery hollows and quiet footpaths, and dotted with the decaying ruins of abandoned churches. The light here takes on an eerie clarity, and even the buildings are different to others in Kent with small, squat churches and secretive little houses, that look as if they are trying to

shrink into the landscape and escape your attention. Romney Marsh was originally an expanse of ever-changing saltmarsh and tidal creeks, reclaimed from the sea first by the Romans and then the Saxons – the name is thought to derive from the Saxon 'Rumnea' meaning marsh water.

This walk takes you between two historic marsh villages, starting at **Ivychurch**, where you park by the **Bell Inn**. The inn sits next to St George's Church, built in the 1360s. It's quiet today but it hasn't always been this sleepy. During the Civil War, Cromwell's soldiers slept here and even stabled their horses in the church. In later years, when smugglers roamed the marshes, churches were often used to hide contraband such as tea and spirits. Some of the marsh churches have a ship painted on one of their walls, a symbol that it was a safe place to hide smuggled goods. St George's was certainly used as a hiding place. At one time the vicar was unable to take Sunday service because, according to the sexton: 'pulpit be

---

WHAT TO LOOK FOR ⓘ

In spring you might well hear a raucous croaking noise rising from the ditches in the marsh. It's the sound of the **marsh frog**, known locally as the 'laughing frog'. Twelve were introduced to a garden pond in 1935 and soon escaped into the surrounding marshland.

full o' baccy and vestry be full o' brandy'. In those days tea was so expensive that locals couldn't afford it, so they made their own version with local herbs. During the Second World War the church was used as a secret food store, in case the country was invaded, and lookouts were posted on the towers. Inside the church you can see some stone seats along one wall. These were reserved for the elderly, in the days before churches had pews. It's one explanation for the saying: 'let the weakest go to the wall'.

WHERE TO EAT AND DRINK ⓘ

You're parked close to the **Bell Inn** in Ivychurch where you can get a drink after your walk. Or try the **Rose and Crown** in Old Romney, an atmospheric pub reached by turning right at the main road when you come down to the village.

With the church on your left, walk along the road, pass the **phone box**, then take the footpath on the right. Go diagonally left across this field – keeping the mast on your right. If it's been raining you'll soon notice your boots getting weighed down with thick, heavy clay. It's a reminder that the marshes were once a swampy, unhealthy place to live. Locals used to suffer from 'Kentish ague', or 'Old Johnny', a shivery, malaria type fever. People tried to ward off the disease by wearing a charm necklace. Walk around the edge of the next field, cross over a bridge and continue until you reach **Yoakes Lane**. At the

lane, turn right and follow it all the way to **Old Romney**. Keep an eye out for the sight of a heron overhead. There are plenty on the marshes as they feed in the ditches that lace the ground.

At **Old Romney** you come to the busy main road (**A259**), turn left here and walk down, before turning left again. Take time to stop in Old Romney and visit the church before continuing the walk. It's set back from the road and dates back to the 11th or 12th century. It contains a rare, pre-Reformation stone altar that had been hidden away and was only discovered during restoration work. Altars like this were banned by Edward VI, as they represented undesirable links to the days before the Church in England broke from Rome. He ordered that they all be destroyed. Old Romney was once a busy sea port, but was stranded as more and more land was reclaimed from the sea.

There is now a choice of routes. You can follow **Five Vents Lane** all the way back to **Ivychurch**, or go up the lane, walk around a curved medieval moat and follow the ditch, walking around the field edges and crossing two bridges, to arrive back at **Yoakes Lane**. You can retrace your steps to reach the village, or turn right and continue along Yoakes Lane to the main road. When you reach the road, turn left and walk back to the **Bell Inn** and your starting point.

WHILE YOU'RE THERE ⓘ

Look out for some distinctive local plants. **Marsh mallow plants** grow by ditches and produce soft pink flowers in July and August. The roots of the plant were once used to make sticky sweets – the forerunners of the commercial marshmallows we can buy today. Along the lanes, look for **blackthorn hedges**, that were planted to supply wood to pack the sea walls. So much wood was needed that it became an offence to chop blackthorn without permission. Anyone who was caught doing so had an ear cut off.

Walk 16

In the Footsteps of Charing's Pilgrims

A gentle circuit taking you along the ancient ridge-top track known as the Pilgrims' Way.

•DISTANCE•	3 miles (4.8km)
•MINIMUM TIME•	1hr 30min
•ASCENT / GRADIENT•	98ft (30m) ▲
•LEVEL OF DIFFICULTY•	🏃 🏃 🏃
•PATHS•	Firm field paths and ancient trackways, 3 stiles
•LANDSCAPE•	Wooded tracks and lush fields
•SUGGESTED MAP•	aqua3 OS Explorer 137 Ashford
•START / FINISH•	Grid reference: TQ 954494
•DOG FRIENDLINESS•	Generally good, watch out for horses
•PARKING•	Off High Street and off Station Road, Charing
•PUBLIC TOILETS•	Old Ashford Road in centre of village

BACKGROUND TO THE WALK

Charing might seem like a quaint, rather sleepy village today, but for centuries it was one of the busiest and most important settlements in Kent. It was a convenient stopping place on the medieval pilgrimage route to Canterbury and practically all pilgrims, whether rich or poor, would have stopped here for the night, before setting off the next morning for the last leg of their journey.

Travelling Companions
Medieval pilgrimages were a bit like early package holidays – a way of seeing the world in the company of others, with itineraries taking in churches, holy relics and inns. And, as Chaucer revealed in *The Canterbury Tales* (1387), by the 14th century, pilgrims were often more concerned with enjoying themselves than with any devout purpose. As pilgrims were vulnerable to thieves who lurked in the woods along the way, they tended to group together for protection and, as they travelled, the atmosphere tended to become increasingly festive.

The Pilgrims' Way
The route known as the Pilgrims' Way in Kent, which you follow for much of this walk, was an ancient trackway used as a trading route by prehistoric people. Wherever possible it followed the top of the ridge, avoiding the thickly forested areas and sticky clay lowlands that would be so difficult to negotiate – especially in bad weather. Pilgrims wouldn't, of course, have had the benefit of modern walking boots. While the wealthy would have travelled on horseback, everyone else would have walked – generally wearing traditional pilgrim's clothes of a broad-brimmed hat and long cloak, and carrying a staff and a 'scrip' – a small pouch which held necessities. Better off travellers might also have carried carved charms to protect them on their journey. Anyone undertaking the pilgrimage as a penance would probably have worn a rough, itchy 'hair shirt' as well.

While ordinary pilgrims would stay at inns along the way, bishops and archbishops expected something far grander, so archbishops' palaces were built at several points on the route. There was a particularly fine one at Charing as it was the last stopping-off point before Canterbury.

When the travellers reached the outskirts of Canterbury those on horseback would dismount and walk into the city; others would probably hobble, as no doubt their feet would have been hurting by then. After visiting the shrine of Thomas Becket in the cathedral, the pilgrims would troop off to buy badges to prove that they'd made it – rather like buying a T-shirt or car sticker today. 'Pilgrims do it on their knees', perhaps? Badges were generally decorated with a scallop shell, the symbol of St James of Compostella that is still used by pilgrims today.

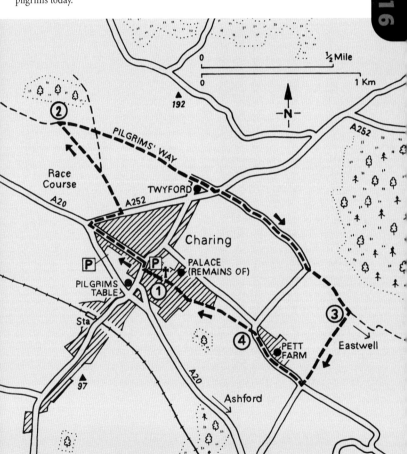

Walk 16 **Directions**

① From the church in the centre of Charing village, walk to the **High Street**, cross over and go up **School Road**. At the roundabout turn right on to the **A252** and then cross the road to follow a public footpath that leads off to the left. Cross a stile and then walk diagonally across a field and through two metal gates. There are two tracks to choose from here – strike out along the left-hand track and make your way up to the trees.

Walk 16

② At the hedge, climb a fence, then turn right and walk along the **Pilgrims' Way**. It's very easy going now, this is a popular route for dog walkers and horse riders. Continue to reach the house called **Twyford**. Where the track ahead forks, go to the right and come on to the A252. Cross over, turn left, walk about 50yds (46m), then turn down the Pilgrims' Way on the right-hand side. Pass a tarmac track on the right and continue to a large tree.

③ The Pilgrims' Way now continues ahead, eventually bringing you to **Eastwell**, the burial place of Richard Plantaganet, illegitimate son of Richard III. Unless you want to walk to Eastwell your route now takes you to the right, down a bridleway. This is an immensely atmospheric lane, with a thick canopy of trees and so old that it has sunk in the middle. Take care if it's wet, as the track is chalky and can get very slippery. At the tarmac road turn right.

④ Just past **Pett Farm** go over the stile by the green gate on the left-hand side. You soon see **Charing church** peeping through the trees. Walk towards the church, crossing another stile. At the bottom of the field turn right through a gap in a thick hedge, that brings you out to a small hut. Walk around the field, along a flagstone path and past a children's play area. Turn right up the fenced path and go into the churchyard.

Orchards and Perfick Villages Around Pluckley

A gentle ramble through the countryside made famous by fictional Kentish family the Larkins.

·DISTANCE·	3 miles (4.8km)
·MINIMUM TIME·	2hrs 30min
·ASCENT / GRADIENT·	98ft (30m) ▲▲
·LEVEL OF DIFFICULTY·	🚶 🚶 🚶
·PATHS·	Orchard tracks and footpaths, some field margins, 17 stiles
·LANDSCAPE·	Apple orchards, pasture and pretty villages
·SUGGESTED MAP·	aqua3 OS Explorer 137 Ashford
·START / FINISH·	Grid reference: TQ 927454
·DOG FRIENDLINESS·	On lead quite a bit, but they'll enjoy this walk
·PARKING·	On street in Pluckley
·PUBLIC TOILETS·	None on route

BACKGROUND TO THE WALK

There can be few such memorable fictional families as the gutsy, lusty Larkins; irrepressible Pop, voluptuous Ma, beautiful Mariette and the gaggle of young, noisy, children. This walk takes you through the heart of *The Darling Buds of May* country, for not only was the television series filmed at Pluckley, but the creator of the Larkins, H E Bates, lived at Little Chart which you pass on your route.

A Prolific Author

Herbert Ernest Bates, to give him his full name, was born in 1905 in Northamptonshire, and moved to Little Chart in 1931 when he and his wife discovered a run down old barn near the village. They converted it to a house, which they called The Granary, and Bates lived there until he died in 1974. Bates worked as a journalist before publishing his first book and quickly established a reputation for his stories about country life in England. During the Second World War, when he served as a Squadron Leader in the RAF, he continued to write, his stories appearing under the pseudonym Flying Officer X. He was astonishingly prolific and one of his most famous books, *Fair Stood the Wind for France* (1944) was written while he was on leave. Other books, like *The Purple Plain* (1947), drew on his experiences in Burma during the Second World War.

The Garden of England

Bates wrote short stories, novels, plays and pieces on gardening and country life. But in everything he wrote, his love of nature shines through, and in the Larkin books he brilliantly captures the beauty of the countryside around Pluckley. There are copses full of bluebells, nightingales in the woods, fields choked with strawberries and trees laden with cherries, cobnuts, pears and plums. Bates also writes of 'miles of pink apple orchards… showing petals like light confetti', and this walk takes you through the heart of some orchards. In spring you'll be able to enjoy the blossom, in autumn you'll see the apples – which, as elsewhere in Kent, often seem to be left to rot on the ground. Apple growing goes back to Roman times and the first large-scale orchards were planted for Henry VIII. Apples were highly prized and even in Victorian times ordinary people could only afford to buy windfalls and bruised fruit.

Far More than Golden Delicious

There are over 6,000 different varieties of apple, and hundreds of types of pears, plums and cherries. Sadly, vast areas of orchard have now disappeared from Kent, due to competition from imported fruit. However people are becoming more interested in eating local produce, so one day you might get the chance to try famous Kentish apples like Beauty of Kent, Gascoyne's Scarlet, Kentish fillbasket and Sunset. As Pop Larkin might have said 'Perfick'.

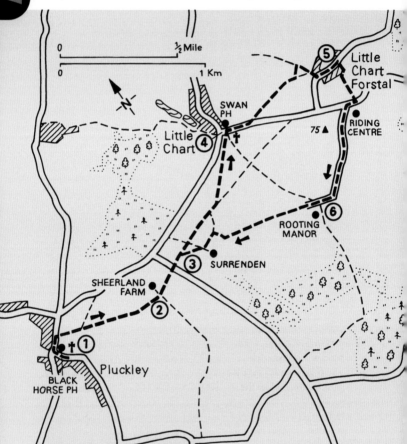

Walk 17 **Directions**

① From the church, turn right and head up to the main road. Walk uphill, turn right by the **Black Horse** car park sign and make for a

gate. Cut across the playing fields and through a gap in the hedge into an orchard. Carry straight on keeping the windbreak on your right-hand side, then maintain direction to cross a metalled track by **Sheerland Farm**.

WHERE TO EAT AND DRINK ⓘ

You pass the **Black Horse** at the start of this walk. It's a large pub and serves everything from soup and sandwiches to Sunday roasts. They serve food every day except for Sunday evening. Alternatively, you can try the **Swan** at Little Chart, which dates back to the 15th century and also offers good pub food.

WHAT TO LOOK FOR ⓘ

Orchards are not the wildlife havens that they used to be, as they are sprayed with insecticide and tend to be densely planted. Still, it's worth keeping a look out to see if you can see any orchard butterflies, such as the small tortoiseshell and red admiral which feed off rotten fruit. Hedgehogs also enjoy fallen apples and sometimes get a bit tipsy if the fruit has started to ferment.

② Continue through the orchards to the road. Bear slightly left, then join a footpath by a brick wall. Follow this, climb a stile and follow the fence line on your left, to cross two more stiles at the bottom.

③ Your route continues ahead, through a gap in a wall, up to another orchard and over a stile. Turn left now and follow the track with the windbreak on your left. Bear right, go over another stile and walk towards a brick wall. Turn right and walk through the orchard to the church. Turn left and go down some steps to join the road opposite the little **Swan** pub.

④ Turn right, then nip over a stile on the left and head diagonally across the field – go to the left of the lone tree. Cross a stile, turn right and walk along the field edge to cross a bridge and a stile. Bear left, then right at the end of a garden to the road – you'll see duck ponds on either side. Follow the tarmac lane, pass a house and, at a waymarker, turn left and walk past the picture postcard village green of **Little Chart Forstal**.

⑤ Nip over a stile on the right, then walk down the right-hand side of the field, climbing two more stiles to reach the road by the riding centre. Turn right, take the first road on the left past the farm and follow it to **Rooting Manor**.

⑥ Where the road bends left, cross a stile by some gates, turn left and walk along the top of the field. Turn right as you pass through the windbreak and walk up the track. Follow the track that leads to the left and go through the orchard, eventually bearing right and up to **Surrenden**. Follow the track on your right, cross a stile on the left and walk up the right-hand side of the field to join the track. Nip over the stile and continue to the road. Cross over, walk through the orchard, then across the playing fields. Turn left and return to the church at the start.

WHILE YOU'RE THERE ⓘ

Pluckley claims to be the most haunted village in England, boasting about a dozen **ghosts**. They range in form from a highwayman, a monk and a gipsy watercress seller, to a Red Lady who wanders through the churchyard, and even a marching band. On top of that there's the furniture in a local inn, which has a habit of moving around by itself.

Walk 18

Natural Drama in Wye

A lovely walk in which you climb the Devil's Kneading Trough for impressive views across chalk downland.

•DISTANCE•	4¼ miles (6.8km)
•MINIMUM TIME•	3hrs
•ASCENT / GRADIENT•	345ft (105m) ▲▲▲
•LEVEL OF DIFFICULTY•	𝝅𝝅 𝝅𝝅 𝝅
•PATHS•	Footpaths, wide grassy tracks and field margins, 6 stiles
•LANDSCAPE•	Dramatic valleys and rolling downs
•SUGGESTED MAP•	aqua3 OS Explorer 137 Ashford
•START / FINISH•	Grid reference: TQ 054469
•DOG FRIENDLINESS•	Can run free in places, older dogs won't like the climb
•PARKING•	Near Wye church
•PUBLIC TOILETS•	Opposite Wye church

BACKGROUND TO THE WALK

As you walk along the North Downs, take a moment or two to think about the land beneath your feet – the chalk was laid down in warm, shallow seas almost 70 million years ago. Today chalk provides an ideal surface for walking, it drains well and doesn't get claggy. However, originally there was a fine mud beneath the sea, made from billions of tiny shells and the remains of small plants – a sort of gloopy, calcium rich soup. The North Downs were formed when movements of the earth's surface forced the Weald of Kent upwards, like a sheet of paper being crumpled. The top of the fold was then eroded, leaving the chalky spine of the Downs exposed.

The most dramatic feature on this walk is the deep gully of the Devil's Kneading Trough, that was formed at the end of the last Ice Age. Kent, unlike most of Britain, was never covered by thick ice sheets, however the ground was almost permanently frozen during the winter months, like parts of the Arctic or Russia today. In the spring, when the thaw set in, the meltwater would gouge deep valleys like this into the chalk.

The Devil's Kneading Trough

As you stand looking across this deliciously green and varied landscape, it's hard to believe that you are looking at something that is artificial. But open chalk downlands only look the way they do because for thousands of years farmers grazed their animals here (► Walk 3). The area around the Devil's Kneading Trough is a precious wildlife reserve and is home to wild flowers such as cowslips, violets, orchids, ox-eye daisies and the wonderfully aromatic wild thyme. Cowslips, so rare today, were once as abundant as buttercups and were strewn beneath the feet of country brides. They used to be known as 'freckled face' because of the orange spots at the base of their petals – spots which Shakespeare, rather romantically, thought gave them their delicate scent. In contrast, the fragrance of wild thyme is due to the presence of an oil called thymol, a natural antiseptic. It was traditionally used in the posy carried by monarchs when they presented Maundy money to their subjects. No, it wasn't there for decoration. It was there to give the monarch some protection from the infectious diseases carried by the poor.

Hastingleigh
MEMORIAL
B
C
▲185
MAST
Hassell
Street
D
A
175 ▲
DEVIL'S KNEADING
TROUGH
RESTAURANT
RIDING
SCHOOL
DEVIL'S
KNEADING
P TROUGH
4
175 ▲
NORTH DOWNS WAY
Wye Downs
5
3
6
WYE
MEMORIAL
CROWN
Brook
—N—
WITHERSDANE
HALL
0   ½ Mile
0   1 Km
2
WYE
1
WC P
NEW FLYING
HORSE INN
▲40
Eastwell

Walk 18

① From the church, walk down **Church Street**, turn left at the bottom, then right along **Cherry Garden Lane**. Keep ahead, crossing over a road and continuing along the track, past a beech hedge.

② The road soon opens out and you continue ahead, past the imposing **Withersdane Hall** and along the footpath. There are flat fields to either side but don't worry, this walk's not all so monotonous – just be patient. At the road, cross over and continue ahead, crossing two stiles to a track ahead – this can get very muddy. At a crossing of tracks maintain direction, and follow a marker post diagonally across a field. Now nip over a stile and come on to the road.

WHAT TO LOOK FOR

Carved into the chalk is the large, creamy white **memorial crown** created by students of Wye College in 1902 to commemorate the coronation of Edward VII. It was illuminated with thousands of tiny lamps on the night of the coronation and also on the Silver Jubilees of George V and Elizabeth II. The crown was camouflaged with brushwood during the Second World War to prevent enemy aircraft using it as an aid to navigation.

③ Walk to the right and you'll soon see a footpath on the left-hand side and a sign saying 'Welcome to Wye Downs'. Walk up the steps, over a stile and continue winding your way up to the top of the hill (still complaining that it's flat?). You get wonderful panoramic views from here. Keep walking ahead to join the road, passing the dramatic gorge known as the **Devil's Kneading Trough** on your right.

④ Cross over, turn left along the road, then join the **North Downs Way** on the right-hand side. Go through the gate and follow the high ground, skirting the valley on the left. The soil here is fine and red, a complete contrast to the usual chalky, flinty soil of Kent. Keep ahead, but don't hurry – the views to the left deserve some attention. After some fine walking you'll reach a bench and observation point above the **Wye Memorial Crown**.

⑤ Take the stile on the right, signed '**North Downs Way**', and walk past a wood on your left. Climb another stile, then continue walking down, following some steps to join a metalled road. Bear left and walk until the land starts dropping steeply away on your right. Turn left to follow the bridleway.

⑥ The route is easy to follow now. Make your way down the rather awkward steps, go through a gate and continue ahead to reach a road. Cross over and take the trackway opposite, through a nursery and greenhouses. At the road, turn left, then go straight ahead at the crossroads. Pass the **New Flying Horse Inn** then walk back up **Church Street** to the start.

WHILE YOU'RE THERE

Not far from Wye is **Eastwell**, one of those forgotten corners of Kent. There's a ruined church here, by a lake that is the burial place of Richard Plantaganet, the illegitimate son of Richard III. He worked as a mason at Eastwell Park after his father's defeat and death at Bosworth Field in 1485. They say his identity was discovered when he was spotted reading a book – an unlikely accomplishment for a 16th-century mason. He was said to be the last of the Plantaganets.

A Stroll to Hastingleigh

A longer walk that takes you to the village of Hastingleigh.
See map and information panel for Walk 18

Walk 19

•DISTANCE•	2½ miles (4km)
•MINIMUM TIME•	1hr
•ASCENT / GRADIENT•	328ft (100m) ▲▲▲
•LEVEL OF DIFFICULTY•	🚶🚶 🚶 🚶

Walk 19 Directions (Walk 18 option)

From Point ④, cross to the **visitor centre**, and then walk behind it to pick up the right of way that runs to the right, along the field edge. When you come to a marker post, go to the right of the wood and, at another marker post, bear left down the track that winds through the trees. You will soon come out at a road, Point Ⓐ. Turn left here and keep ahead. At the second cross-roads, climb the stile on the right-hand corner. Walk along the edge of the field, crossing three more stiles and join a road, Point Ⓑ.

Turn left here and walk up to the large tree on the village green at **Hastingleigh**. Turn right, past the war memorial, and then take the bridleway on the left. At the corner of the woods, where the main track goes ahead, turn left to walk along the field edge. Your path now goes ahead, across the middle of a field, over a stile and into woodland. Go straight through the wood and come out on the road, Point Ⓒ.

Continue walking ahead and at the busier road, cross over and maintain direction up the clear track (there is a radio mast on your left). Walk across the middle of the field to a junction of paths. Go to the right here, along the field edge and come out at a track. Turn left and then bear to the right by the side of the buildings, Point Ⓓ.

Cross a stile on your right, into a small patch of woodland, then nip over another stile. Now head down the pasture, between two patches of woodland, below the ridge on the right. Walk past a riding school, then cross a stile and continue down a grassy track, heading downhill over two more stiles. Walk around the edge of the wood, then bear right and leave the wood behind to follow a grassy track. When you reach the metalled lane turn left and walk down to rejoin the main walk at Point ④.

WHERE TO EAT AND DRINK   ⓘ
On the road by the **Devil's Kneading Trough** is a popular restaurant that serves lunches as well as teas, snacks and cakes. It's conveniently situated to allow you to get your breath back after that climb. Back in Wye there are several places to choose from including the **New Flying Horse Inn** which serves good pub food and beers made by local brewer Shepherd Neame. It has a welcoming log fire in the winter.

Walk 20

Along Appledore's Canal

A walk beside an historic canal, then across fields to a sleepy church.

•DISTANCE•	5 miles (8km)
•MINIMUM TIME•	3hrs
•ASCENT / GRADIENT•	98ft (30m) ▲▲ ▲▲
•LEVEL OF DIFFICULTY•	🚶🚶 🚶🚶 🚶🚶
•PATHS•	Canal banks and field paths, 13 stiles
•LANDSCAPE•	Striking views over Romney Marshes
•SUGGESTED MAP•	aqua3 OS Explorer 125 Romney Marsh, Rye & Winchelsea
•START / FINISH•	Grid reference: TR 956293
•DOG FRIENDLINESS•	Keep on lead where sheep are grazing
•PARKING•	Appledore village car park
•PUBLIC TOILETS•	By recreation ground

Walk 20 Directions

Park in the village car park or on the main street. Walk south down Appledore's main street and past the **Church of St Peter and St Paul**. Although it's about 9 miles (14.5km) from the sea today, the village was a busy port until the 14th century, when the sea started to retreat following extensive reclamation of Romney Marshes. It was a busy trading centre for luxury products such as wool, silk, wine and lace, and was also the hub of a lucrative ship-building industry.

The main street is wide and airy, it reeks of past prosperity and is lined with the homes of former merchants and ship owners. Turn left just before the bridge, go

---

WHILE YOU'RE THERE ⓘ

Steam addicts should love the **Romney, Hythe and Dymchurch Railway**. This miniature railway was built in 1927 for a millionaire racing driver. All the locomotives and carriages are a third of the normal size.

---

through a couple of gates and over a stile and follow the footpath all the way along the **Royal Military Canal**. It's lovely easy walking on a grassy track and you don't have to worry about where to put your feet.

The Royal Military Canal is a reminder that Appledore was once strategically important. The Vikings brought 250 longships here and made the area a base for launching assaults on the surrounding countryside. During the Hundred Years War, French troops raided the coastline, sacked the village and burned down the church. An even greater threat came in the early 19th century, when it looked as if Napoleon's army might invade. Martello Towers were built along the coast and, as a further line of defence, a canal was dug between Rye and Hythe. The idea was that neither cavalry nor artillery would be able to cross the canal, so disrupting any large scale assaults. A military road was built next to the canal, behind an earthen parapet, allowing troops to move about while being protected from

Walk 20

enemy fire. Sluice gates were also added so that, if necessary, Romney Marsh could be flooded.

The canal was never used against Napoleon, as by the time it was completed the threat of invasion had receded. It was, however, used by barges for many years and during the Second World War, when the country was once more threatened by invasion, was fortified again. You can still see pill boxes at various points along your route.

As you walk along the canal you will get great views of the marshes that stretch into the distance on your right-hand side. They are grazed by Romney Marsh sheep, the oldest of all British breeds of sheep. They have rather stocky looking bodies and short legs and are hardy animals, ideally adapted to living in damp conditions. During the summer, sheep farmers like the water level in the ditches to be high, so that their animals cannot stray from the fields, while arable farmers require water to irrigate their crops. So the sluice gates on the canal are used to raise the water level and let water drain out into the ditches.

The route eventually takes you up to a road, where you turn left, go past **Higham Farm** and then go over a stile on the right. Now follow the footpath over the field, heading under the line of pylons and up towards the church tower that peers down on you. Go over another two stiles before coming into the graveyard of Kenardington church. Look behind you for great views over the fields and marshes. Keep to the left-hand side of the graveyard and go over a stile to join the **Saxon Shore Way** that you now follow all the way to **Appledore**.

Keep to the field edge, hop over another stile and join the road. In a few paces you'll see a broken down stile on the right-hand side, which takes you diagonally across the fields, over two more stiles and down into a sunken lane. Go over another stile and walk across the field, maintaining direction to reach the road. Cross over, pop over another stile and walk diagonally across the field, over a small bridge, then ahead over more fields. When you reach a stile on your right, don't cross it, but bear left and follow the Saxon Shore Way as it takes you on to the mound, a Bronze-Age burial site. From here you can see the chimneys of Hornes Place. The house that originally stood here belonged to the local squire and was burned down during the Peasants' Revolt in 1381, when Wat Tyler's men marched through Appledore.

Go downhill, over a stile and a small bridge, then bear left diagonally and go through a gate. Continue to the recreation ground and the main road, where you turn left and walk back into **Appledore**.

From Lenham…

…then fast to Paris?

•DISTANCE•	3½ miles (5.7km)
•MINIMUM TIME•	2hrs 15min
•ASCENT / GRADIENT•	49ft (15m)
•LEVEL OF DIFFICULTY•	
•PATHS•	Field tracks and roads, can be muddy in places, 19 stiles
•LANDSCAPE•	Patches of farmland traversed by railways
•SUGGESTED MAP•	aqua3 OS Explorer 137 Ashford
•START / FINISH•	Grid reference: TQ 522899
•DOG FRIENDLINESS•	Keep on leads, not good for dogs that don't like trains
•PARKING•	Centre of Lenham
•PUBLIC TOILETS•	None on route

BACKGROUND TO THE WALK

Put away your anorak and notepad – you don't have to be a train spotter to do this walk. For although it might not be the most scenic walk in this book, it gives you a real insight into the way Kent's landscape is being shaped in the 21st century. And as you'll almost certainly see high speed trains, as well as major engineering works, children should love it.

The Channel Tunnel Rail Link

The walk starts from Lenham, an ancient village settled since Saxon times. Many buildings date back to the 13th century and the town square is extremely photogenic. Once you're out of the village, you swiftly leap several centuries as you come to the main railway line that runs from London to the coast. If you look back as you make your way towards the sewage works, you may well get a great view of a Eurostar train clattering through the countryside on its way to Paris. Then you continue through pasture and past sturdy old farmhouses, until you come right up to the new Channel Tunnel Rail Link – Britain's first new mainline railway in over a century. This line, which is successfully carving up even more of Kent's already beleaguered countryside, will run for 69 miles (111km) from the mouth of the Channel Tunnel near Folkestone to London Waterloo. It is the final part of a transport project first conceived in the 19th century.

The French Thought of it First

For hundreds of years the only way to travel between England and France was by boat. The idea of linking the two countries by a tunnel under the English Channel was initially proposed by a French engineer in 1802. His idea was for a tunnel that would be used by horse-drawn vehicles. The tunnel would be lit by oil lamps and an artificial island in the middle of the Channel would provide a staging post for changing the horses. Napoleon was interested in the idea and although war with Britain meant he couldn't go ahead with it, the concept would not go away. Throughout the 19th century various other tunnel projects were put forward and Channel Tunnel companies were formed on both side of the Channel. In the early 1880s, the invention of a boring machine allowed private companies to commence drilling, and a pilot tunnel 6,000ft (1,829m) long, was bored from England. However, the tunnel was controversial as many people felt it represented a threat to national security and the project was stopped.

After the Second World War the idea was revived and, after some false starts, drilling of the 31 mile (50km) tunnel finally went ahead. It was officially opened in 1994. When the new high speed rail link is finished the present journey time from London to the Channel Tunnel should be halved.

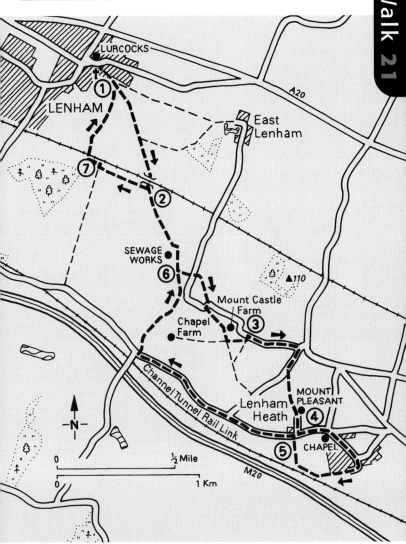

Walk 21 Directions

① From the parish church in Lenham walk across the churchyard and squeeze through a kissing gate.

Follow the track diagonally across the field, then cross a stile. Continue walking in this direction, crossing fields and two more stiles, then walk under the broad arch of the railway bridge.

Walk 21

② Turn slightly left, then walk to the bottom corner of the next field where you cross a stile and a tiny wooden bridge. Bear left to the sewage works, up the ramp, then over the stile. Turn sharp right and head to the bottom of the field. Don't follow the Stour Valley Walk signs but walk round the edge of the field, over a stile, then cross three more stiles, walk up to the top of the field, then down towards the farmhouse, where you cross a stile on to a track. (Yes, it would be quicker to walk straight over to the farmhouse, but you'd be straying from the right of way.)

③ Walk to the right, then turn right again. Just past a fruit producer's sign, hop over a stile on the left. Head uphill to a gate, through some scrub and turn left at a tarmac lane. Just past **Mount Pleasant**, a converted dovecot, go to the right down a fenced track.

④ At the road, walk to the left to a tiny former chapel, then take the lane on your right. This now sweeps past a farm and down to the site of

the new **Channel Tunnel Rail Link**. Bear to the right, keep within the fenced area and go through a gate and over a stile. Turn right, then walk back to the road.

⑤ Turn left and continue along the road for ¾ mile (1.2km), past some cottages until you turn up a footpath on the right, which leads back to the sewage farm. Look up for a great view of the cross that has been cut into the hillside.

⑥ At the sewage farm turn right, pop over two stiles and a little bridge. Your route now goes left, over another stile and back to the railway arch. When you reach the railway turn left and walk parallel to the railway line.

⑦ Cross two little bridges and a broken down stile then cross the railway line. Walk down to the bottom of the field, through a gap in the fence and continue ahead along the left-hand edge of the field. You cross one more bridge then walk diagonally across the field and back to the church.

Bowled Over in Sutton Valence

A popular walk ending at the grave of the man who changed the modern game of cricket.

•DISTANCE•	3½ miles (5.7km)
•MINIMUM TIME•	2hrs
•ASCENT / GRADIENT•	148ft (45m) ▲▲ ▲ ▲
•LEVEL OF DIFFICULTY•	🚶🚶 🚶🚶 🚶🚶
•PATHS•	Field edges and quiet lanes, 12 stiles
•LANDSCAPE•	Orchards, oast houses and rolling fields
•SUGGESTED MAP•	aqua3 OS Explorer 137 Ashford
•START / FINISH•	Grid reference: TQ 812492
•DOG FRIENDLINESS•	Good, though they'll need to be kept on lead
•PARKING•	Village streets – it can get pretty crowded
•PUBLIC TOILETS•	None on route

BACKGROUND TO THE WALK

You might expect a man who revolutionised the sporting world to be buried somewhere grander than a sleepy little churchyard in rural Kent. But you'll find just such a grave at the end of this walk; it's the grave of John Willes. Never heard of him? Listen in then.

The Early Days

John Willes was a local man and a keen cricketer. Kent has always been at the forefront of English cricket and the first recorded inter-county match was played between Kent and Surrey in 1709. Willes, keen to perfect his batting skills, used to practice in a barn, getting his sister Christina to bowl to him. It was then the convention to bowl under-arm, but Christina used to wear a crinoline and the hooped skirts got in the way, making it difficult for her to send the ball very far. She came up with the idea of flinging the ball over her head instead and Willes was surprised to find that it travelled about twice as fast.

A 19th-century Pitch Invasion

Willes decided to adopt the style himself and, in a match at Maidstone in 1807, he bowled over-arm for the first time. The spectators were horrified and invaded the pitch, apparently pulling up the stumps to prevent him continuing. After that the MCC ruled that balls should always be bowled under-arm, but Willes refused to give up his unconventional style.

In 1822 in a match at Lords, Willes bowled over-arm and was given 'no ball'. He threw a rather undignified tantrum, chucked the ball on the ground and flounced off the pitch, declaring that he would never play cricket again. In the end of course, the style was adopted and Willes continued to play, acting as coach to another great Kentish cricketer Alfred Mynn. Willes died in 1852 and is buried in St Mary's churchyard in Sutton Valence, which you reach by crossing the busy road at the end of this walk. His is the first grave you see when you enter the graveyard. It's inscribed with the words: 'patron of all manly sports and the first to introduce round arm bowling in cricket'. His sister isn't mentioned.

The Willes were not the last Kentish people to play a part in cricketing history. When the Ashes were first brought to England, they were initially kept in an urn on the mantelpiece, in the home of the captain in Cobham. One morning a maid apparently knocked them over and the Ashes spilled into the fireplace. She grabbed a handful of ash from the fire and popped it into the urn. The ashes from that Kentish fireplace are still said to sit at Lords today.

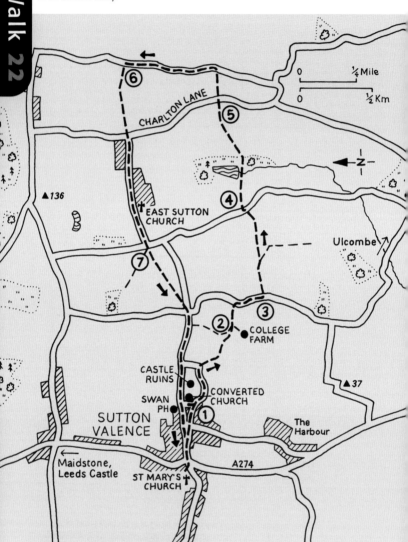

Walk 22 Directions

① From the converted church in the centre of the village, turn right down the lane, then left at the

bottom to pass the **ruined castle**. Dating back to the 12th century, it was built to guard an important medieval trading route. Continue to the end of the lane, and then bear right. Where the road bears

Walk 22

downhill, continue walking straight ahead along the lane. There are plenty of orchards here and it's a lovely sight in the spring when the blossom is out.

② Come on to a surfaced area by **College Farm**. Keep walking ahead until you reach the road and then turn right. Go downhill passing a pond on the right-hand side. At a bend, nip over a stile to follow the footpath on the left.

③ Stroll along the top of the field to another stile, passing a pond on the right-hand side. Go through a gap in the hedge, over a metal gate and on to the road. Turn left and, after a few paces, take the footpath on the right.

④ Cross a stile into the field and follow the fence line past a tumbledown wall and up to the woods ahead. Continue to some

iron railings, which you follow into the woods. Pass a pond on your left, cross a small bridge and continue ahead until you pop over a stile into a field. Bear slightly left, go through a gate, then head towards the treeline and turn right to cross a stile on to the road.

⑤ Cross the road, climb another stile then continue ahead over two more stiles to the next road. Turn left to follow the lane uphill for 600yds (549m). Just past a house turn left by a wooden gate onto a public bridleway.

⑥ Your route sweeps down now, over a stile and follows the field edge to take you on to **Charlton Lane**. Hop over a stile, cross the road and walk up the road ahead – signed 'Sutton Valance'. Follow the road past **East Sutton church** and, at another road, climb another stile into a field.

⑦ Take the obvious path towards some trees and at a waymarker go straight on along the clear track. Continue to the treeline in front of you, then cross a stile in the corner of the field to join the road. Walk straight on now and back to Sutton Valence village. To reach **St Mary's Church** walk through the village, cross the busy **A274** and take the footpath immediately ahead. Return to the village centre to finish your walk.

Walk 23

Oasting Around in Bethersden

A circular walk along quiet lanes and past oast houses.

•DISTANCE•	4½ miles (7.2km)
•MINIMUM TIME•	2hrs 30min
•ASCENT / GRADIENT•	82ft (25m) ▲ ▲ ▲
•LEVEL OF DIFFICULTY•	🚶 🚶 🚶
•PATHS•	Tarmac lanes, badly signposted field tracks and one muddy farmyard, 17 stiles
•LANDSCAPE•	Agricultural land with oast houses, a good walk in summer
•SUGGESTED MAP•	aqua3 OS Explorer 137 Ashford
•START / FINISH•	Grid reference: TQ 929403
•DOG FRIENDLINESS•	Number of stiles and poultry farm makes this less than ideal for dogs
•PARKING•	On street parking in Bethersden
•PUBLIC TOILETS•	None on route

BACKGROUND TO THE WALK

'…everybody knows Kent. Apples, cherries, hops, and women.'

That was Mr Jingle in *The Pickwick Papers* (1836). I don't know where he got the women from, but there's no doubt that Kent has long been noted for its fruit orchards and hop gardens. And it is the cultivation of hops that has given the county its most distinctive feature – the oast house. With their warm red brickwork and distinctive white cowls, they dot the landscape like foaming pints of beer and you'll pass several of them on this walk.

The Introduction of Beer

Hops, a relative of the cannabis plant, were originally grown only as a herb and weren't farmed commercially until the 16th century. In medieval times the favoured English drink was ale, which was thick and sweet and flavoured with herbs and spices. Beer, which gets its distinctive bitter taste from hops, is thought to have arrived in the 15th century with Dutch merchants, who drank it all the time. For some reason the authorities frowned upon it and during the reign of Henry VI the use of hops in drink was made an offence. Even in the 16th century, by which time beer had become a popular drink, people still disapproved of it. Henry VIII forbade his brewer from using hops and one physician wrote '…it makes a man fat as shown by the Dutchmen's faces and bellies'.

The first English hop gardens were established in Kent. The soil here was suitable, there was a ready supply of wood to make the hop poles on which the crop could climb, and the farmers were wealthy enough to afford the high initial outlay required to establish the gardens. Hop gardens are easily spotted, with poles supporting an aerial lattice of strings. The plants produce cones, which are harvested by machine today, although it used to be labour intensive work as they were traditionally picked by hand. Whole families from the East End of London would travel to places like Bethersden to harvest the hops, treating the work as a holiday. Once picked, the cones are dried in oast houses before they are ready for use. You can make a stab at guessing the age of an oast house; the earliest types were rather like large barns, or rectangular in shape, while the Victorians built round oast houses as they thought this helped to dry the hops more efficiently. Modern oast houses are rather severe and rectangular. The local hop industry has declined in recent years due largely to competition from cheaper imports.

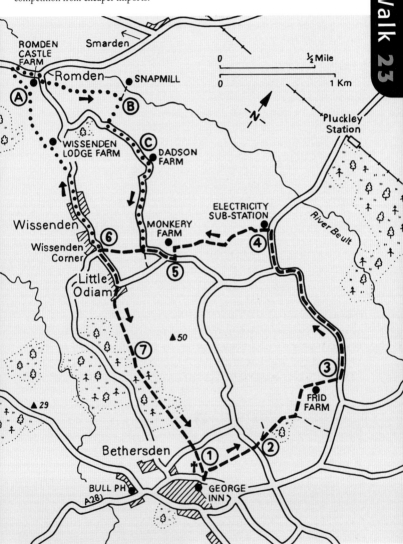

Walk 23 Directions

① From the churchyard, follow the footpath, then take the right-hand path over a stile and down a track.

After another stile, go straight ahead up to some trees. Nip over a stile and cross the road.

② Climb the fence by a metal gate and walk through a salvage yard.

Walk 23

At a fork, keep to the right and take the narrow track through the trees. Cross a stile, walk straight ahead along the field edge, then go left at a marker post. At the bottom of the field bear right, then immediately left, and walk ahead between two ponds. Go through the gate and cross the farmyard.

③ Follow a tarmac drive to the road (private planes land here and you'll pass a sign saying 'danger – stop, look aircraft'). Turn left and continue for ¾ mile (1.2km) to the main road and turn right. Turn left at the **electricity sub-station**. Reach a field and walk diagonally left towards the first lone tree, then continue to the hedge.

④ Cross a bridge, go through some scrub and over a stile. Turn left at the high wire fence, then go through the high metal gate – you might have to push very hard to get it open. Another gate brings you into a slimy poultry yard. Walk around the edge of the pond and then go through another gate. Cross two more stiles, and then turn left in pasture where you go right, up the track.

> ### WHERE TO EAT AND DRINK ℹ
> The **George Inn** in Bethersden serves snacks, Sunday roasts and a range of home-cooked food, as well as teas and coffees. Outside the village on the Ashford Road is another pub, the **Bull**, which also serves meals and real ales.

> ### WHILE YOU'RE THERE ℹ
> **Smarden** is a feast of historic timber-framed and white weatherboarded houses, a sight that makes visitors reach for their cameras. If you get time to visit, do stop and look at the pagan carving in the local church. It is thought to be a fertility symbol, or a sexual war goddess, placed there to repel the 'evil eye' and protect worshippers in the church.

⑤ Walk to a junction, turn right and follow the road as it bears right then, on the corner, clamber over a broken down stile and follow a public footpath to the left. Walk diagonally across two fields to **Wissenden Corner**.

⑥ Turn left, walk to **Little Odiam** and take the footpath to the right. After two more stiles and a small bridge you reach a marker post. Bear right and walk diagonally towards the woods.

⑦ At another marker, cross a tiny bridge and two stiles, then walk straight across the field. Reach another bridge and stile where the track goes at a diagonal. Cross a bridge in the wood and then take the distinct track on the left. At another small bridge and stile you emerge from the wood and cross pasture, then head towards the bottom left-hand corner of a field. Cross another field to a line of trees and continue to a tarmac path. Continue ahead over two more stiles to return to the churchyard.

> ### WHAT TO LOOK FOR ℹ
> Bethersden was once famous for its production of **Bethersden marble**, which was used in many local churches and the cathedrals at Rochester and Canterbury. In fact it wasn't real marble, but a stone formed from the compressed shells of freshwater snails. They inhabited this area around 300 million years ago when it was a lush, freshwater swamp. The stone came in many colours and could be polished to look like marble. Local people once laid slabs of it over the fields, making causeways so that pack-horses could transport wool to neighbouring markets.

A Loop from Wissenden Corner

An extra loop makes a figure of eight across fields.
See map and information panel for Walk 23

•DISTANCE•	6½ miles (10.4km)
•MINIMUM TIME•	3hrs 30min
•ASCENT / GRADIENT•	131ft (40m)
•LEVEL OF DIFFICULTY•	👫 👫 👫

Walk 24 Directions (Walk 23 option)

From **Wissenden Corner**, Point ⑥, turn right, walk up the road, and pass a white house and some oasts. Just before the corner take the footpath to the left, cross a stile and go diagonally across the field to the left of a farm. Go round the right-hand side of the wood, pass some houses, then walk straight ahead. Keep walking in the same direction to reach an oak tree. Go slightly right, through a gate to **Romden Castle Farm**. Cross the stile on to the road, Point Ⓐ.

Much of this land was once owned by Richard Lovelace (1618–57). A Cavalier and a poet, he was reputed to be the handsomest man in England. Although he wrote many poems, he's best known for just two lines of verse which come from one of his earliest works, *To Althea, from Prison* (1642); 'Stone walls do not a prison make, Nor iron bars a cage'.

Richard Lovelace wrote these words while he was in prison in the gatehouse of Westminster Palace. He had been sent there as punishment for supporting the 'Kentish Petition'. This was a document that had been drawn up by the county's gentry, urging the King and Parliament to try to resolve their differences and so avert civil war. It was, as we know, unsuccessful – and when the war did break out and Lovelace was released he fought on the side of the King. When Cromwell came to power, Lovelace lost all his land around Bethersden.

Turn right and walk along the road. Where it bends, follow it round to the right, signed 'Bethersden'. Soon after there's a gap in the hedge by a broken footpath sign. Go through this to head straight across the field to another gap in a hedge. Meet another track and bear left to **Snapmill**. At a junction of tracks, Point Ⓑ, turn right. Keep the field boundary on your left-hand side – the track bears left then right, then joins another track that takes you to **Dadson Farm**, Point Ⓒ. Turn right to a group of old houses. Keep on the road to **Monkery Farm**. Take the track to the right-hand side and walk down to **Wissenden Corner**. Continue, following the route of Walk 23, through Point ⑦, and back into **Bethersden** village.

Walk 25

Wine and Port at Small Hythe

Discover a lovely wooded valley on this short walk.

•DISTANCE•	3 miles (4.8km)
•MINIMUM TIME•	2hrs 30min
•ASCENT / GRADIENT•	82ft (25m) ▲ ▲ ▲
•LEVEL OF DIFFICULTY•	🚶 🚶 🚶
•PATHS•	Field edges, footpaths and some sections of road, 22 stiles
•LANDSCAPE•	Fertile fields and pasture, one steep sided valley
•SUGGESTED MAP•	aqua3 OS Explorer 125 Romney Marsh, Rye & Winchelsea
•START / FINISH•	Grid reference: TR 892303
•DOG FRIENDLINESS•	Good, can often run free, though not near road
•PARKING•	Tenterden vineyard car park
•PUBLIC TOILETS•	Vineyard visitor centre

Walk 25 Directions

This walk starts from Tenterden vineyard. The Romans first introduced vines to England and by Tudor times English winemaking reached a peak, when local vineyards were producing almost 3 million bottles each year. After the dissolution of the monasteries production declined, to the extent that English wine was looked upon as something of a joke. However, the industry was revived about 40 years ago and is flourishing today. This area of Kent is ideal for growing grapes as it has well drained south facing slopes and a warm, dry climate.

From the vineyard car park, walk left towards the **telephone box**, and then turn right and walk between two gardens to cross a stile. Follow the hedgerow to the bottom of the field. Continue across the next field, cross a bridge and a stile. Walk across the bottom of the field keeping the hedgerow on your right, and then maintain direction crossing two more stiles to a yellow waymarker. The track now runs along the side of a hedge, through a metal gate and across the field to a stile. Continue in the same direction crossing another stile, and then walk up the side of a field. Go over two more stiles, then where the track splits, go straight ahead to go over another stile and a bridge. Climb the steps cut into the bank and walk around the edge of a pond, then follow the footpath ahead. Your route now takes you over a stile and a small bridge, across a field and up to a gate.

Continue through the gate, go straight ahead and, at another gate, take the steps over a bridge and up the side of a hill. Continue ahead at a crossing of tracks, and then cross two bridges before you come to a marker post. Go left along the side of a wood. Turn right at the next marker post, pop over a stile and walk diagonally across the field.

Walk 25

WHILE YOU'RE THERE

From Tenterden you can take a trip on the **Kent and East Sussex Railway** – a steam railway that runs between Tenterden and Northiam in East Sussex. It's a good way of seeing the lovely, lush countryside of two counties.

Continue to cross a stile, then turn right past the gates at **Belcot Farm**. Walk past the farm and follow the track into the wood.

Your way now leads past gardens on the outskirts of Tenterden. This is a busy town with a wide, tree-lined **High Street**. It became prosperous during the 15th century, thanks to the local wool industry. Weekly markets were held here when sheep would be driven down the High Street. At this time Tenterden was a maritime town, standing at the head of an inlet. It was considered important enough to be made an associate of the Cinque Ports (a town which received special privileges, in return for providing men and ships to form part of the country's defensive force).

At the road in the housing estate, cross over and walk ahead, pass a pond and then nip over a stile on your left. Follow the track over a bridge and across the field, following the line of the overhead cables. At a waymarker, go down some steps, across the stream, over the stile and carry on ahead through the field. Pass a small pond and head for the stile beside the electricity transformer. Cross the stile, turn right and continue to the main road. Turn left, walk past a house called **Ormsby**, and then turn left after the white timbered house and follow the footpath over a stile. Walk ahead through an old orchard, then turn right by a caravan and walk up the track, and over a stile to a fence by the bottom of the gardens. Turn left here and walk down the track, with young trees on either side, to cross a stile in the fence in front. Walk diagonally towards a large tree, and then on, over two more stiles, before turning right along a road. Continue to a pond, cross a stile, go through the field, through a gate, over two more stiles and join the road. Go through a gate across the field, turn right at another gate and descend some steep steps on to the road – be careful here as there's no pavement. Follow the road downhill towards **Small Hythe** and your starting point. Small Hythe was once a busy port and a prosperous shipbuilding centre – hard to grasp today, as the coast is miles away.

WHERE TO EAT AND DRINK

Tenterden vineyard has a good café and restaurant that serves traditional sponge cakes, scones and light meals. In summer you can sit outside and enjoy the views. You can of course buy wine in the shop and there are free tastings.

WHAT TO LOOK FOR

Smallhythe Place, opposite Tenterden vineyard, is one of those photogenic places featured in many brochures. This 16th-century timber-framed house once belonged to the harbour master and part of the grounds formed the ship repair dock. Today most people know the house for its associations with the actress Ellen Terry (1848–1928). Ellen first appeared on the stage at the age of eight and by the late 19th-century was regarded as London's leading Shakespearean actress. She lived at Smallhythe Place from 1899 to 1928 and the house, now administered by the National Trust, has displays of memorabilia.

Walk 26

The Mistress of Benenden

Discover the history of a famous girls' boarding school and its connection with a popular children's rhyme.

•**DISTANCE**•	4 miles (6.4km)
•**MINIMUM TIME**•	2hrs
•**ASCENT / GRADIENT**•	180ft (55m) ▲▲▲
•**LEVEL OF DIFFICULTY**•	🏃🏃 🏃🏃 🏃
•**PATHS**•	Grassy tracks, woodland paths and field margins, 19 stiles
•**LANDSCAPE**•	Lush open fields, parkland and an imposing old school
•**SUGGESTED MAP**•	aqua3 OS Explorer 125 Romney Marsh, Rye & Winchelsea
•**START / FINISH**•	Grid reference: TR 808327
•**DOG FRIENDLINESS**•	Good, they can run free for much of walk
•**PARKING**•	By village green in Benenden
•**PUBLIC TOILETS**•	None on route

BACKGROUND TO THE WALK

> *'Lucy Locket lost her pocket*
> *Kitty Fisher found it,*
> *Not a penny was there in it*
> *But a ribbon round it'*

They might have been immortalised in a nursery rhyme, but Lucy Locket and Kitty Fisher were certainly not the innocent young girls that we tend to imagine. Quite the opposite – they were a couple of celebrated 18th-century courtesans who used their distinctive talents to work their way into high society.

Appointment with Casanova
Kitty, whose real name was Catherine Maria, worked as a milliner but her more exotic exploits brought her to the attention of a wider public. Casanova made a point of meeting her when he came to London and she even had her portrait painted by Sir Joshua Reynolds – today it is on display at Petworth House. Kitty inspired many songs and verses: a country dance was named after her, and her namesake appears in *The Beggar's Opera* (1728).

The Upwardly Mobile Kitty
The nursery rhyme we know today – there are several versions of it – was sung in both England and America, usually to the tune of *Yankee Doodle Dandy*. Kitty was such a skilled social climber that in 1766 she married John Norris, the grandson of the Admiral of the Fleet, who brought her to live at Hemsted, the fine manor house at Benenden. Such a marriage would have represented a real achievement for a working class girl and would have given her wealth, security and respectability. Kitty quickly settled into her new role as lady of the manor. She was very popular locally and generous to the poor people of the village. Unfortunately, she didn't get much chance to enjoy her new life as she died of smallpox just four months after her marriage. She was buried in the local church dressed, in keeping with her last wishes, in her best ball gown.

An Exclusive Girls' School

Hemsted was visited by Elizabeth I in 1573, when she stayed there as a guest of Sir Thomas Guldeford. She planted a walnut tree in the grounds but sadly it's no longer there as it fell down in the 19th century. The house you see today is very imposing and looks Jacobean with its tall chimneys and stone-framed windows. However it dates back to only 1860, when the original Hemsted was rebuilt. In 1924 it came to the attention of some teachers looking for a suitable location for a boarding school and today Hemsted houses Benenden School, one of the most exclusive girls' schools in the country. Among its many well-known former pupils is Princess Anne, the Princess Royal. Kitty Fisher would surely have approved.

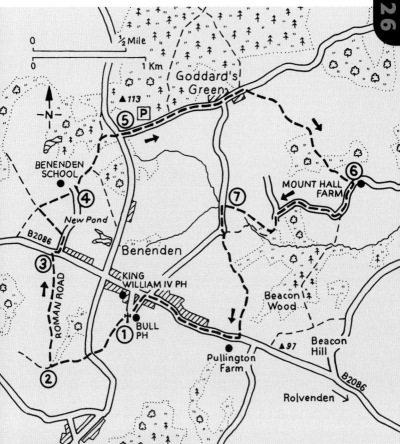

Walk 26 Directions

① From the church turn right, follow the footpath and go over the stile. The route now continues over three more stiles as you cross the fields and the road to join a grassy track. Go through the gate at the bottom, then the wooden gate on your right.

② You're now following the course of an old Roman road. It's still dry and firm – those Romans knew about road building. Walk up the left of the field, climb the stile at the top and continue through another

Walk 26

field, keeping ahead at some waysigns. It's tranquil here with rolling pasture and mature trees. Pass a pond, then nip over the stile in the hedgerow. Walk towards the houses and climb a stile in the top left-hand corner of the field. Turn right and continue until you reach the main road.

③ Turn right, cross by the sign for **Benenden School** and follow the tarmac road. Turn left, head along the bottom of the playing fields, go over a stile and then follow the fence line on your left. Don't cross the stile in front of you, instead turn right and walk towards the school. Keeping the school on your left, walk ahead to cross a stile by a house.

④ Cross the driveway and maintain direction with the newer parts of the school on your left, then nip over a stile into a field and go left towards the wood. Bear right to cross a stile, then follow the track, going past one stile before crossing another by a wooden gate. Follow the fence line, climb a stile and continue to the driveway. Turn right and walk to the main road.

⑤ Cross over, continue to **Goddard's Green** and then take the second public footpath on your right. At the house, nip over the stile and keep going left. Your route now leads across fields, over an overgrown stile and through a copse, which you leave by another stile. Turn right and follow the marker to **Mount Hall Farm**.

 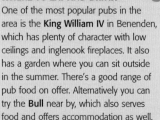
⑥ Turn right, follow the road on to a track, then continue through the woods to a tarmac road.

⑦ Turn left along the road and, at the top of the rise, nip over a stile. Take the track on the right, go through a gate and across the field to climb another stile. Walk down the track, over another stile and into the woods. Cross a wooden bridge, then walk to a group of trees. Turn right and continue to climb a stile by the road. Turn right and walk back into Benenden.

Gardener's Delight in Sissinghurst

A lovely, easy walk to the famous garden created by Vita Sackville-West and Harold Nicholson.

•DISTANCE•	3 miles (4.8km)
•MINIMUM TIME•	2hrs
•ASCENT / GRADIENT•	33ft (10m) ▲ ▲ ▲
•LEVEL OF DIFFICULTY•	🚶 🚶 🚶
•PATHS•	Well-marked field paths and woodland tracks
•LANDSCAPE•	Gentle Kentish countryside dotted with oast houses
•SUGGESTED MAP•	aqua3 OS Explorer 137 Ashford
•START / FINISH•	Grid reference: TQ 814409
•DOG FRIENDLINESS•	Excellent, though do keep on lead
•PARKING•	On street in Frittenden
•PUBLIC TOILETS•	Sissinghurst

BACKGROUND TO THE WALK

Eat your heart out Charlie Dimmock. Charlie's distinctive water features may be well known in Britain, but her fame is nothing compared to that other English gardener Vita Sackville-West (1892–1962), whose horticultural flair led her to create the garden at Sissinghurst Castle, one of the most famous gardens in the world.

A Connoisseur's Garden

Vita moved to Sissinghurst in 1930 with her husband, Sir Harold Nicholson. She was born at Knole, the family seat in Kent, but although she was the only one in the family who really loved the place, she was unable to inherit because she was a woman. When she saw Sissinghurst she realised that this was an estate she could make her own; even though it was in such a terrible condition that it took five years before she and her husband had mains water or electricity.

Although styled as a castle, Sissinghurst was in fact an Elizabethan mansion owned by the Baker family (related by marriage to the Sackvilles). When the family fortune declined the house began to deteriorate, and in 1756 it became a prison camp for French prisoners of war. Conditions in the camp were appalling and at the end of the war the house was in such a state that much of it was demolished. The house continued to be neglected until the Nicholsons bought it and set about restoring it and creating the now famous garden.

Literary Connections

The most striking part of the house is the tall brick tower that you see as you walk across the fields from Frittenden. Vita used it as her study and did all her writing here: poems, novels and gardening articles. One of the few visitors she allowed into this isolated place was Virginia Woolf. They met in 1922 in London and had a relationship that would have scandalised society, but of which both their husbands were understanding. Virginia wrote her novel *Orlando* (1928) as a tribute to Vita and her love for the family estate, Knole.

The house is interesting and still home to the Nicholson family. But it's the garden that people come to see, ten separate gardens in fact, all linked together. Harold Nicholson was a gifted garden designer and created the beds and enclosures at Sissinghurst, while Vita tended to concentrate on the planting, choosing old-fashioned roses, as well as herbs and clematis. The most famous garden is the White Garden, which Vita filled entirely with white flowers and pale foliage. If you do this walk early in July and visit Sissinghurst you should find that the magnificent white rose, at its centre, is in flower. Apparently family weddings are always held on the second Saturday in July to coincide with its blooming.

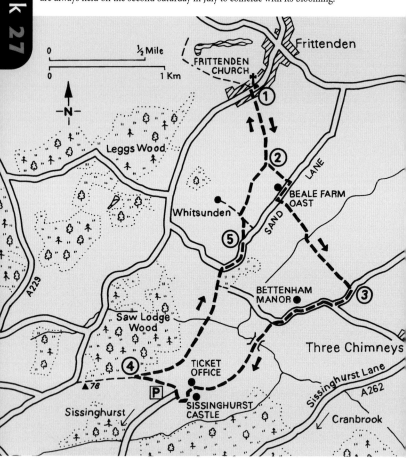

Walk 27 **Directions**

① With your back to **Frittenden church** turn right, then left down a pathway by the hall. Cross a stile and walk straight ahead over the field, through a gate and across another field. Go through a kissing gate then straight ahead again – it's clearly marked. At a gap in the hedge cross a little wooden bridge and make your way to a telegraph pole, where you branch left.

② Nip over a stile, go across the next field, over another stile and on to a tarmac lane to turn right past **Beale Farm Oast**. At the next house, turn left and walk up the

Walk 27

WHAT TO LOOK FOR ⓘ

The **herb garden** at Sissinghurst contains over 100 varieties of herbs, varying from kitchen herbs like oregano, coriander and rosemary to more unusual herbs like woad. Although the flowers of woad are yellow, the leaves of the plant can be made into a blue dye. It was once used by the ancient Britons to paint their faces.

track until you pass an old barn. Turn right just after the barn, continue ahead over two more stiles and eventually cross a footbridge to the right of a clump of trees. Walk a few paces left, continue in the same direction up the edge of the field, then turn left again to cross another bridge. Scramble through some scrub and follow the path ahead to another stile and on to a road.

③ Turn right, then right again at the road junction. You pass **Bettenham Manor**, turn left up a bridleway, over a bridge, then pass **Sissinghurst Castle** (still home to Vita Sackville-West's heirs), keeping the building on the left. Walk up to the oast houses, then bear left around them, past the ticket office and up the driveway. Turn left, then right and walk by the side of the car parks to a stile. Cross into a field, then bear right in a few paces to cross a stile by some cottages.

④ Turn right, walk back past these cottages, and then bear left along the path through the trees. Continue ahead along a tree-lined track, cross a stream and keep following the bridleway. When you come to a road, cross over and walk up **Sand Lane**.

⑤ Eventually reach a stile on the left-hand side which you cross and then head diagonally across the field to another stile in the fence ahead of you. Continue diagonally, passing a dip in the field. Keep the spire of the church in front of you and walk ahead to cross another stile. The path is clear ahead, then veers to a telegraph pole where you go left, heading for the spire of **Frittenden church**. Cross a bridge and walk back into the village the way you left.

WHILE YOU'RE THERE ⓘ

The nearby village of **Cranbrook** was the capital of the Kentish wool industry in the 15th century, and consequently was extremely prosperous. Many of the houses you can see today were the homes of the local weavers. The local church, St Dunstan's, sometimes called the 'Cathedral of the Weald', was built with money from the cloth trade.

WHERE TO EAT AND DRINK ⓘ

There's a tea room at **Sissinghurst**, which you conveniently reach about half-way round the walk. It serves cakes, scones and snacks. Otherwise, try the **Bull Inn** in the village of Sissinghurst, which serves everything from bar snacks to full meals. It also has a large garden.

Walk 28

Hawkurst's Smugglers

A circular walk from Hawkhurst, once the haunt of smugglers.

•DISTANCE•	5 miles (8km)
•MINIMUM TIME•	2hrs 30min
•ASCENT / GRADIENT•	246ft (75m) ▲▲▲
•LEVEL OF DIFFICULTY•	🚶🚶 🚶🚶 🚶
•PATHS•	Woodland tracks and field margins, 25 stiles
•LANDSCAPE•	A mix of open fields, dense woodland and orchards
•SUGGESTED MAP•	aqua3 OS Explorer 136 The Weald, Royal Tunbridge Wells
•START / FINISH•	Grid reference: TQ 763305
•DOG FRIENDLINESS•	Can run free but might object to all those stiles
•PARKING•	Car park in Hawkhurst
•PUBLIC TOILETS•	None on route

BACKGROUND TO THE WALK

The name Hawkhurst once struck fear into the hearts of Kentish people, for it used to be the headquarters of the vicious Hawkhurst Gang, a notorious band of smugglers who terrorised the area in the mid-18th century. Prior to the 13th century, smuggling didn't exist; not because people were more honest, but because there were no customs duties. Around 1300, Edward I introduced a customs levy on wool, which was England's primary export and in great demand in Europe, particularly for the Flemish weaving industry. Although the rates were low at first, they soon increased as the Crown needed money to fight the Hundred Years War with France (1337–1453). The woollen industry continued to grow in importance, particularly when Flemish weavers, encouraged by Edward III, came to Kent and settled in the Weald, bringing with them their skills in cloth making.

Early in the 17th century, the export of wool was made illegal, and smuggling increased. Wool smugglers were known as 'owlers', as they used to hoot like owls to communicate in the dark. Although the number of customs officers gradually increased, smuggling became more profitable and port officials could often be bribed. When the illegal export of wool became punishable by death, the smugglers began to arm themselves.

At first smugglers were seen as Robin Hood figures, helping people to acquire goods at prices they could afford. As well as wool, they would also smuggle goods such as spirits, silks, tea and tobacco. However, as gangs became more organised they also became more sinister and began to intimidate local people. The most ruthless of all was the Hawkhurst Gang who controlled all the smuggling on the south coast from 1735 to 1749. Farmers were forced to lend them horses and informers would be beaten or murdered. The gang was so powerful that they could assemble 500 armed and mounted men within an hour. They operated from the Oak and Ivy pub in Hawkhurst, where, apparently, a tunnel once ran from the pub to Tubs Lane near Cranbrook (so called because of the tubs of brandy that used to be seen floating in the water). In 1822, a cave the gang once used as a storehouse was discovered in Soper's Lane. It wasn't until 1747, when the people of Goudhurst formed a militia and managed to kill several smugglers, that anyone showed any resistance. When the gang viciously tortured and murdered two informers two years later, several smugglers were captured and hung and the Hawkhurst Gang gradually lost its influence.

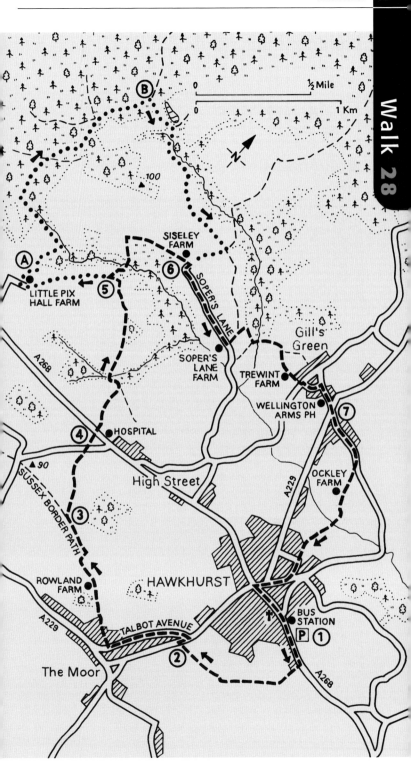

Walk 28

Walk 28 Directions

① Leave the car park by the **bus station**, turn left up the main road, cross over then follow the public footpath that runs down to the right. Continue to climb a stile by a metal gate and bear right, following the hedge across the field and past a pond. Now follow the track through woodland, over three stiles and into rough pasture. Hop over a stile to join the road.

WHAT TO LOOK FOR ⓘ

St Laurence's Church in Hawkhurst dates back to the 14th century, but it was badly damaged by a 'doodlebug' during the Second World War and has been much restored. A window commemorates Sir John Herschel (1792–1871), the English astronomer who lived in Hawkhurst.

---

② Turn right, follow the road and then cross to go left along **Talbot Avenue**. Pass the village green, take the footpath on your right (the **Sussex Border Path**) and follow it into the woods to **Rowland Farm**. Walk past the farm, bear right to the top of the field, crossing a stile on your left, and then follow the waymarker up the field.

③ Where the track splits, leave the **Sussex Border Path** to go right and through an orchard. Hop over a stile at the top and follow the track as it bears left, then go right over two more stiles. Cross a lane and go across another field, over a stile and on to the **A268**.

④ Cross the road, climb a stile, walk through the hospital car park, and then nip over two more stiles to follow the track through woods. After another stile, head sharp left and go back into the woods. Follow the track, which soon swings to the right over a stream, cross two more stiles, stroll across the field to another stile and re-enter the woods. Another stile takes you into a field where there's an obvious track leading over a bridge. Your route now goes left along the edge of the trees.

⑤ Nip over a stile, then follow the clear farm track on your right to reach the buildings of **Siseley Farm**.

⑥ Walk past the farm, and then climb a stile to take the footpath on the left by **Soper's Lane Farm**. Walk ahead, then turn right at the second gate, where you now cross two stiles as you make for the bottom corner of the field. Follow the track to your left, cross a stream and head towards the gap in the fence. Bear right to **Trewint Farm**, cross the road and turn left, then right, to reach the **Wellington Arms**.

⑦ Cross the busy **A229** here and walk ahead until you come to a byway on the right. Follow this past **Ockley Farm** and up into the outskirts of **Hawkhurst**. Turn right, walk to the crossroads and then turn left to return to the car park.

WHILE YOU'RE THERE ⓘ

You might think that pine trees belong in the far north, but **Bedgebury National Pinetum** contains the national collection of conifers, with over 6,000 trees in landscaped grounds. The first plants for the pinetum were raised at Kew and were planted here in the 1920s, adding to earlier plantings that had been carried out by Viscount Marshall Beresford of Bedgebury (1768–1854), who fought at Waterloo. He planted the Old Man of Kent, the tallest tree in Kent, which stands 165ft (53m) high.

Through the Conifers at Bedgebury

A longer walk gives you time to ponder with Hawkhurst's cleverest resident.
See map and information panel for Walk 28

•DISTANCE•	6½ miles (10.4km)
•MINIMUM TIME•	3hrs
•ASCENT / GRADIENT•	443ft (135m) ▲▲ ▲ ▲
•LEVEL OF DIFFICULTY•	🚶 🚶 🚶

Walk 29 Directions (Walk 28 option)

The name Sir John Herschel (1792–1871) may not trip off your tongue, but he is well known to astronomers. He lived and worked in Hawkhurst for 30 years and during that time discovered over 3,000 double, or binary, stars (two stars revolving around a common centre). Not content with that, Herschel was also one of the pioneers of photography. He invented the process of reproducing photographs on sensitised paper, and was the first to use the terms 'positive' and 'negative' in the context of photography. He is buried in Westminster Abbey, next to Sir Isaac Newton.

At Point ⑤ continue walking along the wide track that leads towards **Little Pix Hall Farm**. Walk through the farm, Point Ⓐ, and take the first track on your right past some cottages. Follow the concrete track as it meanders uphill, then turn left. The track runs along the edge of the wood and then bears to the right. This is a bridleway, so watch out for horses if you have a dog with you.

The right of way now turns right and continues to a junction of two tracks. Take the path on the right and continue to walk through the woods, passing silver birch trees and young conifers. You'll eventually reach a junction where two tracks lead off to the left. Ignore these and continue ahead on the right of way.

Carry on down the slope and, at a signpost, take the track on the right, Point Ⓑ. Now walk past a large pond (you'll hear the ducks quacking through the trees as you pass) then take the large track that slopes down to your right. It's used by vehicles and can get very muddy. You'll see feed bins, set out by game keepers, along here for game birds such as pheasants and partridges. When you come down to a crossing of tracks turn right and walk down to **Siseley Farm**. Turn left here to rejoin Walk 28 at Point ⑥ and follow it back to **Hawkhurst**.

WHERE TO EAT AND DRINK   ⓘ

The **Oak and Ivy** is a 14th-century pub slightly out of the centre of Hawkhurst on the A268. It serves baguettes and a good selection of bar meals, as well as teas and coffees. At Gill's Green there's the **Wellington Arms**, which also serves meals, real ales and has a coffee lounge.

Walk 30

The Banks of Bewl Water

Birdwatchers should enjoy this walk to the South's largest reservoir.

•DISTANCE•	3 miles (4.8km)
•MINIMUM TIME•	1hr 45min
•ASCENT / GRADIENT•	427ft (130m) ▲▲ ▲▲ △
•LEVEL OF DIFFICULTY•	🚶 🚶 🚶
•PATHS•	Woodland paths, field edges and farm tracks, 17 stiles
•LANDSCAPE•	Fields, woods and an enormous stretch of water
•SUGGESTED MAP•	aqua3 OS Explorer 136 The Weald, Royal Tunbridge Wells
•START / FINISH•	Grid reference: TQ 711322
•DOG FRIENDLINESS•	Good, can run free in places
•PARKING•	Car park on A21, north of Flimwell – charges can apply
•PUBLIC TOILETS•	At car park

Walk 30 Directions

There's always something relaxing about walking near water, so this is a walk not to be rushed. It takes you right down to the banks of Bewl Water, a huge reservoir that forms the largest expanse of freshwater in southern England.

Park at the car park on the **A21** north of Flimwell, by the junction with the **B2079**. Turn right and walk along the slip road to reach a large green barn. Turn left on to the public footpath, go through the gap in the fence and walk along the back of the cottages. Pass through a gate into a field and follow the hedgerow on your left. When the hedgerow ends, carry straight on across the field in front, heading for the row of single trees and follow these down to the woods at the

> **WHERE TO EAT AND DRINK** ⓘ
> In Ticehurst try the **Cherry Tree Inn** which has loads of sandwiches and other bar snacks. They also have an extensive blackboard menu and serve real ales.

bottom. Cross a stile, go over a small wooden footbridge, nip over another stile and follow the obvious track into the woods.

The footpath bears slightly right and slopes uphill. At a crossing of paths go to your right, continue to a small clearing and then go back into the woods. As you walk you'll pass conifer trees. Conifer woods aren't as attractive to wildlife as deciduous woods, as the trees form such a thick canopy the light can't penetrate. In turn, wild flowers can't grow on the forest floor and as there are no plants to attract insects – and in turn birds – there is a rather sterile environment. Cross over a stile and sleeper bridge, then continue along the track with a wooden fence on your left. Nip over a stile, cross the road and go through the gate on the other side.

You can now see **Bewl Water**. Follow the track with the water on your right, go through the trees and up to a grassy area that would make a good picnic spot. Bewl Water was created between 1973 and 1975 to

Walk 30

supply the growing demand for water in the south east. Its construction meant that a large area of woodland was cleared and several historic houses dismantled – and apparently rebuilt elsewhere. The Bewl was dammed and the surrounding valleys flooded. When it was finished 6,886 million gallons (31,300 million litres) of water were needed to fill the reservoir. Like all large areas of water, Bewl attracts a wide variety of bird life. Local birdwatchers come here to see great crested grebes, herons, Canada geese, wigeon, gadwall, tufted ducks, moorhens, coots and pochards. Pochards are winter visitors to Britain, many of them coming here from northern Scandinavia and Russia. Flocks of several thousand of them can gather on large areas of water. If you're wondering how on earth you recognise a pochard, the male has a glossy chestnut head, black chest and light grey wings.

Continue following the track, go through a gate and walk up the bridleway into an open field. The route now goes across another field and on to a farm track – you'll see a radio mast on the hill. Follow this track to join the road, turn right, walk up the road, then hop over a stile on your left. Turn right and walk towards the fence line to

WHAT TO LOOK FOR   ℹ

The woods around Bewl Water support a variety of birdlife and, if you're lucky, you might see a **nuthatch**. These perky little birds look rather like small woodpeckers. They have a cinnamon coloured chest, dove grey wings and a thick black line across their eyes. They can perform the rather nifty trick of walking down trees head first, and like to eat nuts such as acorns, hazel cobs and chestnuts.

another stile. Now your way takes you over two small bridges and two more stiles to a white house. Go up a few steps, cut into the bank, and cross a stile on to the road. Turn right and walk down the road. At the sign for **Dale Hill Hotel and Golf Club** turn left, walk past the hotel and continue until you come to a track on your left. Walk down this, then clamber over a stile and turn right. Now follow the hedgerow round to your right, around one of the greens, then go straight ahead into the trees and cross another stile. Walk diagonally across the field, nip over the stile and follow the hedgerow on your right before walking between two copses and over a stile on to the road, where you turn left.

Continue to **Birchenwood Oast**, turn left and follow the track, going over a stile, past a conifer plantation and over another stile. Turn left and walk down the edge of the wood, continue straight ahead to a signpost with three directional arrows. Go immediately left, descend a steep slope and walk through the woods, following the **Sussex Border Path** until it meets the B2087. Cross over and continue to follow this waymarked walk until you come to a junction of paths. Turn right and walk back to the car park and your starting point.

WHILE YOU'RE THERE   ℹ

Bewl Water is a great place to bring children as there are plenty of activities around the lake. There's a woodland playground and you can also go windsurfing or mountain biking. The **Outdoor Centre** offers courses, covering everything from sailing and canoeing to climbing. You can also take trips on the *Frances Mary* passenger ferry. Cruises operate from Easter to September.

A Herbal High Around Goudhurst

A short but rewarding walk around one of Kent's highest villages.

•DISTANCE•	3 miles (4.8km)
•MINIMUM TIME•	1hr 45min
•ASCENT / GRADIENT•	164ft (50m) ▲▲▲
•LEVEL OF DIFFICULTY•	🚶 🚶🚶 🚶🚶🚶
•PATHS•	Well-marked field paths, short sections of road, 12 stiles
•LANDSCAPE•	Superb views of the Weald throughout, take your camera
•SUGGESTED MAP•	aqua3 OS Explorer 136 The Weald, Royal Tunbridge Wells
•START / FINISH•	Grid reference: TQ 7233776
•DOG FRIENDLINESS•	Good but keep on lead as there are lots of grazing animals, stiles are particularly high and might be hard to negotiate
•PARKING•	Car park in Goudhurst behind duck pond
•PUBLIC TOILETS•	None on route

BACKGROUND TO THE WALK

This is the sort of walk that you can do again and again. It's varied, lovely at any time of the year and offers great views from the start – for very little effort. Even better, it's unusually well signposted – so thumbs up to the sensible farmer (or farmers) who help to keep it so enjoyable.

Traditional Medicine

Goudhurst is a very pretty village, though sadly blighted by heavy traffic. It's one of the highest villages in Kent – hence those great views. The village is dominated by St Mary's Church, which has an eye-catching memorial to members of a prominent local family – the Culpepers. The family pop up all over Kent (Henry VIII's fifth wife, Catherine Howard was a Culpeper) but the most famous member of all was Nicholas, the physician and author of *The English Physician Enlarged*, or *The Herbal* which was published in 1653.

Healing Herbs

At that time the working class was moving away from the countryside and into the rapidly growing industrialised towns and cities where there were more job opportunities. In these unfamiliar, urban environments they could no longer gather the traditional herbs they used to make their own medicines. They became increasingly reliant on herbalists and apothecaries – who frequently exploited them. Nicholas Culpeper (1616–54), who trained as a herbalist in London, was conscious of the gulf between the lifestyle of his wealthy family and the majority of the population. He tried to help by letting his poor customers have their herbal medicines at low prices; always tried to use cheaper, local herbs in his remedies, and would even tell people where they could go to gather the herbs themselves. He wrote *The English Physician Enlarged*, or *The Herbal* so as to make his remedies accessible to as many people as possible. Although some of his concoctions sound rather outlandish today, many of the herbs he recommends are still in use. One of his remedies was a 'decoction' of that distinctive Kentish plant hops, which he said: 'cleanses the blood, cures the venereal disease and all kinds of scabs'. Herbalists today say that hops are a mild sedative and contain a natural antibiotic.

Gardens or Fields?

In 1341 the Archbishop of Canterbury decreed that the vicar of Goudhurst should receive an annual tithe which included 'pears, onions, and all other herbs sown in gardens…'. Hops were an important local crop even then and this started a fierce legal dispute over whether hops were grown in gardens or fields, with the vicar, of course, arguing that they were grown in gardens. Although the vicar lost his case, people in Kent still talk about hop gardens – rather than the hop fields that are found in the rest of England.

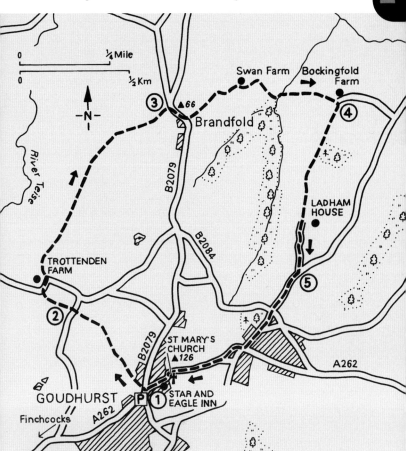

Walk 31 Directions

① From the car park turn left, cross the road and walk up it opposite the duck pond. Just past the bus shelter turn left and follow the public footpath, crossing a stile and walking downhill. There are outstanding views over the **Weald** from here – the whole countryside seems to have been sprinkled with oast houses. It's the sort of view you usually only get after a steep climb.

Keep going down, past two large trees and walk to the bottom right of the field where you hop over a stile and into a narrow, tree-lined path. Follow this to a stile, go over a little bridge and on to a tarmac minor road.

② Cross over to another stile and continue ahead over pasture to a tennis court. Skirt round the left of this and, after another stile, come on to the road, where you turn right. Turn left through the gate signed 'Private Road' into **Trottenden Farm**. Follow the track that winds to the right, go past a pond, over a stile and walk ahead along a fenced track and across pasture. The ways are so clearly marked on this walk that you can't really go wrong. Hop over a stile by a gate and continue ahead to another stile. At a fence post walk to the right, round the edge of a meadow, cross a wooden bridge, nip over another stile and into woodland. Walk uphill to another stile and continue ahead to a road.

> ### WHERE TO EAT AND DRINK ℹ
> The ancient **Star and Eagle** Inn is right next to the church (a story tells that it was once connected to the church by a secret passage). It serves Sunday roasts, light meals, baguettes and teas and coffees. There are also some tea rooms and several other pubs in the village.

> ### WHILE YOU'RE THERE ℹ
> Just by Goudhurst is **Finchcocks**, a Georgian manor house, set in its own parkland, that has hardly altered since it was built in 1725. It is now a museum of musical keyboard instruments. There are chamber organs, harpsichords, pianos and clavichords, and you can hear them being played when the house is open.

③ Turn right and at a corner turn left up a public bridleway. Turn right at a cottage and come down into a field. At a post by a hedge turn right and go downhill. At the bottom cross some water and then veer left, walking uphill towards a farmhouse.

④ Just before the farm outbuildings turn right along a track that runs by a hedge. As you walk you will see fruit trees peeping through the gaps in the hedge. Eventually pass the parkland of **Ladham House** on the left and then come to some concrete bollards. Continue walking to join the road.

⑤ At the road turn right, and walk up to the **B2084**. Cross over and walk along the road immediately in front of you. At a junction keep to the right and continue to reach the main road. Turn right here and you can now see **St Mary's Church**. Follow the road and walk back into the village.

> ### WHAT TO LOOK FOR ℹ
> One local tale concerns marks on the outside of the 13th-century **St Mary's Church**. They are said to have been made by archers sharpening their arrows before going into battle at Agincourt in 1415. It is impossible to say whether this is true or not, however, inside the church is a brass commemorating John Bedgebury who is thought to have been one of the English knights who fought at Agincourt. There's certainly a good chance that he came to the church before heading off to war.

Ancient Sites of Aylesford

This walk takes you to some of the most ancient sites in England.

•DISTANCE•	5 miles (8km)
•MINIMUM TIME•	2hrs 30min
•ASCENT / GRADIENT•	230ft (70m) ▲▲▲
•LEVEL OF DIFFICULTY•	林林 林林 林
•PATHS•	Field paths and ancient trackways, some road, 12 stiles
•LANDSCAPE•	Mix of ancient and industrial landscapes, superb viewpoint
•SUGGESTED MAP•	aqua3 OS Explorer 148 Maidstone & the Medway Towns
•START / FINISH•	Grid reference: TQ 729590
•DOG FRIENDLINESS•	Very few off lead sections plus proximity to very busy roads means this is not too dog friendly.
•PARKING•	Aylesford Friary
•PUBLIC TOILETS•	Aylesford Friary

BACKGROUND TO THE WALK

You will never be alone on this walk, no matter what time of year you do it. Everywhere you go, you will be surrounded by the spirits of the past. For although it is entwined in busy roads and peppered with warehouses and factories, Aylesford is not the modern place it appears to be; in fact it is one of the oldest continuously occupied sites in England.

Thousands of years ago, neolithic people made this area their home. The North Downs offered safety, as well as a plentiful supply of flint for tools, and the river could be easily forded at low tide. Aylesford was settled by the Romans and was the site of an important battle in which the Jutes, Hengist and Horsa, defeated native Britons in AD 455. Alfred defeated the Danes here in AD 893 and Normans built the village church.

Neolithic people were surprisingly sophisticated – certainly not the savages that we once believed. Not only did they use tools, but they also farmed the land and herded animals. They created trackways, such as the route we call the Pilgrims' Way today, and traded with one another, not just within Britain but overseas too. Neolithic people also had religious beliefs and they built elaborate tombs, probably for the most important members of their community. You pass one of these tombs on this walk, built, as was the tradition then, on high ground. It is known as Kit's Coty House, the name meaning the house ('coty') of Kit, or Catigern, an Iron-Age leader who was once thought to have been buried there. However, this site is far older than that. Often called Kent's Stonehenge, it dates back 5,000 years. It consists of three enormous upright stones with another huge stone resting on top. It's almost impossible to imagine just how they got the stones up here, let alone got them into place. This stone portal would once have been buried under a mound of earth and was a communal burial site, probably for religious leaders.

Close by, is Little Kit's Coty House, the remains of another neolithic burial chamber that is possibly even older than Kit's Coty House. All you can see now are a mass of half buried stones. They are sometimes called the Countless Stones, because each time you count them you are said to arrive at a different number. We will probably never fully understand the significance of these sites to early humans, but they're a fascinating glimpse into the lives of the people that once walked the same tracks that you're following today.

Walk 32

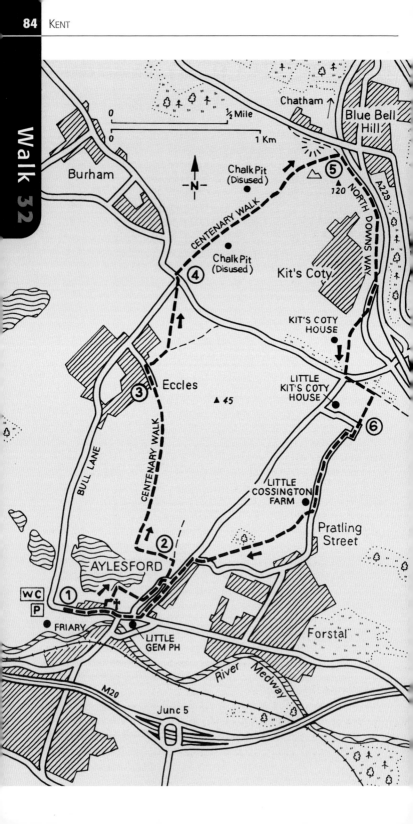

Walk 32

Walk 32 Directions

① From the car park in Aylesford turn right towards the village, cross the road and join a raised pathway. Walk up some steps and go round by the graveyard, then follow the track to a tarmac road. Go left here, then left again to follow the **Centenary Walk**.

② At the marker post take the left-hand track and walk left around the field until you come to some scrub. Walk through this, turn right and walk ahead to a patch of woodland. Keep this on your right and continue ahead, ignoring any tracks on the right. Eventually the path bends left into **Eccles**.

③ Turn left along a residential street then take the public footpath opposite No 48. Pop over a stile and take the left-hand track around the edge of the field. Go over a stile and bear right, then cross another stile just to the left of an electricity pylon. Now keep ahead across the fields, going over five more stiles until you reach **Bull Lane**.

④ Turn right on to the **Pilgrims' Way** – here a very un-medieval main road – and then left until you reach some cottages. Cross over and walk up the **Centenary Walk**

footpath. Follow this as it winds up to **Blue Bell Hill**, where there's a final steep ascent. After crossing a stile at the top, the route goes right along the **North Downs Way**. (However, do take a detour left to enjoy the eye catching views from **Blue Bell Hill** car park.)

⑤ Keep following the **North Downs Way** until you join a road. Don't cross the bridge, but continue along the road. A sign on the right directs you to **Kit's Coty House**, an incongruous site in this busy landscape. Walk down to a busy road junction, turn left and join the **Pilgrims' Way** – it's on the corner, by the M20 sign. (**Little Kit's Coty House** is on the main road further down to the right.)

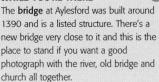

⑥ Follow the lane, then take the first track you come to on the right. This brings you to a road which you follow ahead. Just past a farmhouse take a stile on the right and walk diagonally across the field. Cross another stile and bear right towards a patch of woodland. Continue over another stile and find a gate in the bottom right-hand corner. Go through this and turn right along the road. Turn left at the junction, then right to return to the start.

Along the Medway

A relaxing walk beside the banks of the Medway from West Farleigh.

•DISTANCE•	4½ miles (7.2km)
•MINIMUM TIME•	2hrs
•ASCENT / GRADIENT•	262ft (80m)
•LEVEL OF DIFFICULTY•	
•PATHS•	Field paths and river walkway, some road, 12 stiles
•LANDSCAPE•	Lush pasture and busy riverbank
•SUGGESTED MAP•	aqua3 OS Explorer 148 Maidstone & the Medway Towns
•START / FINISH•	Grid reference: TQ 721526
•DOG FRIENDLINESS•	Keep on lead near livestock, popular with local dog owners
•PARKING•	Good Intent pub car park – ask landlord's permission
•PUBLIC TOILETS•	Teston picnic site

BACKGROUND TO THE WALK

When William Cobbett (1763–1835) travelled through England in 1823 he fell in love with this part of the Medway, describing it as 'the finest seven miles that I have ever seen in England… across the Medway, you see hop gardens and orchards two miles deep…'. Although there are far fewer hop gardens or orchards today, the area is still well worth exploring. This walk takes you through the little village of West Farleigh, then across lush pasture before bringing you down to the banks of the Medway, the river that runs through the heart of Kent.

The Medway rises in Sussex then flows through the Weald of Kent and into the county town of Maidstone, before making its way up to Rochester where it flows into the Thames Estuary. The river valley's fertile soils have made it an important focus of settlement for thousands of years and many neolithic burial chambers have been found in the valley. The river's name is thought to derive from the Celtic word 'medu' or mead, meaning that the waters were sweet and clean. The Romans, who called the river 'Fluminus Meduwaeias', also settled by the river and the sites of several villas have been discovered on its banks, including one at East Farleigh.

The Medway was an important transport route for many years, although it was only navigable from Maidstone, and was an important factor in developing the local economy. Kentish corn, iron, wool and timber would regularly be taken along the river to be sold in London. Another important product of the Medway valley was ragstone. This was quarried by the Romans to build the walls of London, used by the Normans for the Tower of London, and later used for such buildings as Westminster Abbey and Eton College. It's even used today, by the Environment Agency, in the construction of tidal defences.

East and West Kentings

A distinction is often made between men born east and west of the Medway. Those from the east are known as men of Kent, while those from the west are Kentish men (to confuse the matter some sources claim that it's the other way around). It seems to date back to the early Saxon settlers who divided themselves into East Kentings and West Kentings. Whatever the truth is, it serves to show just how important the river was to the life of the Kentish people.

Walk 33

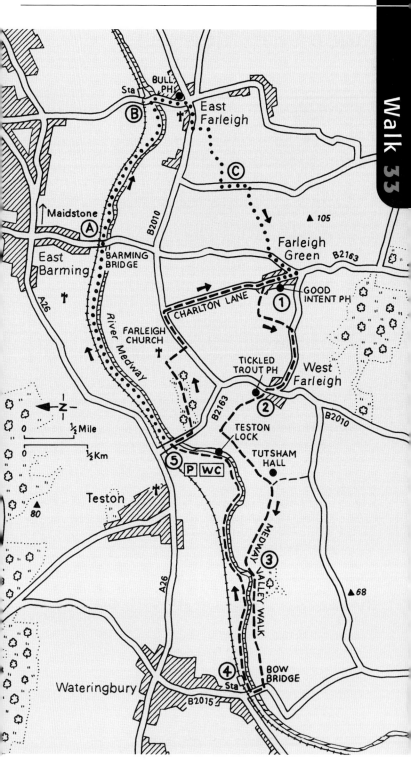

Walk 33

Walk 33 Directions

① From the **Good Intent** pub at Farleigh Green go left, then left again down the footpath. The right of way has been diverted so, just before the garage, veer left then follow the path in front of you. Nip over a stile on the left and cross the field (ignore another stile), keeping the fence on your right-hand side until you reach the main road. Turn right and walk to the road junction, then cross to the **Tickled Trout** pub. Resist the temptation for early refreshment and go through a kissing gate on the left, immediately before the pub.

WHAT TO LOOK FOR
In the spring some marshy areas by the river are used by frogs for spawning. **Frogs** are no longer the common creatures they once were, partly because the wetlands they inhabit are fast disappearing. Frog spawn should never be collected and taken away – even if you've got a garden pond.

② Walk down the field, cross a stile and bear right. Follow the path down to the bottom of the field and cross the stile that lies to the right of the wartime pill box. Turn left and pass **Tutsham Mill Cottages**, then follow the signs ahead for the **Medway Valley Walk**. Bear to the right in front of **Tutsham Hall** and then walk through the farmyard. Go over a cattle grid, cross a stile into a field and follow the Medway Valley Walk right down to the river bank.

③ Nip over the stile and into the woods, then walk through the trees until you come to a small bridge that crosses a particularly muddy piece of ground. Keep walking by the river and then bear to the left to cross a small stiled bridge into the next field. Make for the right-hand corner of the field, cross a stile and squeeze through a kissing gate. Continue ahead until you reach the road, where you turn right and cross **Bow Bridge**.

④ Immediately after crossing the bridge turn right, walk down to the river and join the tow path. You can't get lost now, just keep following this path, going through several gates until you come to **Teston Lock**, a pleasant, lively affair with a rushing weir. Go under the stone bridge, over a stile and on to the road.

⑤ Turn right and cross the bridge, then walk up some steps on the left and follow the wooded track until you cross a stile and come into a field. Walk ahead to cross another stile, which brings you out by **Farleigh church**. Turn right and walk down to the main road. Walk left along this road then turn right up **Charlton Lane** and back to the pub at Farleigh Green.

WHERE TO EAT AND DRINK
The **Tickled Trout** pub at West Farleigh is very popular and serves meals and snacks, as well as tea and coffee. You can also try the **Good Intent** pub at Farleigh Green.

WHILE YOU'RE THERE
Maidstone is the county town of Kent and although it now has a truly ghastly tangle of roads at its heart, it does have some historic buildings worth investigating. There's the former Archbishop's Palace, built in the 14th century for archbishops travelling between London and Canterbury; All Saints Church on the site of a Saxon place of worship, and the College of All Saints, which was originally a medieval college of priests.

And on to East Farleigh

A longer walk to see East Farleigh's ancient bridge.
See map and information panel for Walk 33

•DISTANCE•	6½ miles (10.4km)
•MINIMUM TIME•	2hrs 30min
•ASCENT / GRADIENT•	262ft (80m) ▲ ▲ ▲
•LEVEL OF DIFFICULTY•	🚶 🚶 🚶

Walk 34 Directions (Walk 33 option)

From Point ⑤ the walk continues along the banks of the **Medway**. However, cricket lovers might first like to take a trip into **Teston** (pronounced Teeson) as it used to be the home of Alfred Reader, a traditional cricket ball manufacturer. The company was established in 1808 and balls from here were used in both Test and County matches.

As you walk along the river keep an eye out for the jewel-coloured dragonflies that frequently dart across the water. If you're really lucky you may even see a kingfisher. The railway line is on your left-hand side the whole way but the peace of the riverbank is only occasionally broken by the clatter of a passing train.

Go past **Barming Bridge**, Point ⒶA, and continue walking all the way to the old bridge at East Farleigh.

East Farleigh bridge is reckoned to be one of the finest medieval bridges in England. Made of local ragstone, it's extremely picturesque, with four pointed arches, and is so narrow that cars can only cross it in single file. During the Battle of Maidstone in 1648, during the Civil War, the Royalists tried to hold the town against the Parliamentary forces, led by General Fairfax. They expected the attack to come from the north, but Fairfax took them by surprise and sent his men round the outskirts of the town, then over East Farleigh bridge. His troops then marched up to Maidstone from the south, capturing the town for Parliament.

The path brings you out by a level crossing, Point ⒷB. Turn right and cross the bridge, taking great care as it is extremely busy and narrow. Walk into **East Farleigh**, and then turn right at the pub and walk along the main road. Soon after this you will see some oast houses where, on the left-hand side of the road, there is a public footpath sign. Follow this across the fields until you come to a stile which brings you out on to a road, Point ⒸC. Turn left, walk up the road, then turn right at a public footpath sign and walk up some steps. Follow the path until you come to a stile that you cross into a field. Climb another stile and turn left to walk along the track. You will soon come back to **Farleigh Green** which is on the right.

Walk 35

Holy Tricks at Boxley

A short but energetic walk to the ridge of the North Downs that also takes in an historic abbey.

•DISTANCE•	3 miles (4.8km)
•MINIMUM TIME•	2hrs
•ASCENT / GRADIENT•	508ft (155m) ▲▲▲
•LEVEL OF DIFFICULTY•	🚶🚶 🚶🚶 🚶
•PATHS•	Tracks, lanes and field paths, can be muddy, 5 stiles.
•LANDSCAPE•	Steep scarp of North Downs, and glorious views over Kent
•SUGGESTED MAP•	aqua3 OS Explorer 148 Maidstone & the Medway Towns
•START / FINISH•	Grid reference: TQ 773589
•DOG FRIENDLINESS•	Older dogs won't like steep climb, can be very muddy
•PARKING•	On street in Boxley
•PUBLIC TOILETS•	None on route

Walk 35 Directions

Boxley sits at the foot of the North Downs, squeezed in between a mesh of modern roads. It must always have been a busy place as it is just off the ancient Pilgrims' Way.

Start your walk at the church, cross **Boxley Road** in front of the **Kings Arms** and take the public footpath to the right of the pub. Pass between the cottages on either side into open fields. After the first field, cross an arable field to a stile in the far hedge. Nip over this and turn left down the slope, with the strip of woodland to your left. At the foot of the field you come to the boundary

WHILE YOU'RE THERE ⓘ
For an insight into country life in Kent from the 18th-century onwards, visit the **Museum of Kent Rural Life**, at Cobtree, Sandling. It's got loads of historic buildings including huts in which hop pickers used to live, an old farmhouse, reconstructed cottages, herb gardens and much more.

fence of the **Channel Tunnel Rail Link**, which cuts through the countryside here.

Turn right and cross a stream just above the newly constructed concrete banks. Ahead of you is a flight of timber steps, which takes you on to a new road bridge over the railway line. Pass through a gate, cross the bridge and go down another set of steps. Ahead of you, at the foot of the slope, is the ivy-covered wall of **Boxley Abbey** grounds. Turn right and follow the edge of the field back towards the road, coming on to it again at the house called '**Curlews**'. Turn left and descend to the crossroads at **Abbey Gate**, where you turn left again. Just past a row of cottages you can see the arch of the abbey grounds. You can't go in as it is privately owned, but you can see a beautiful 13th-century barn that once belonged to the estate.

Founded in 1146, Boxley Abbey was Cistercian and was once one of the most wealthy, and infamous, abbeys

Walk 35

in the country. The monks here devised an elaborate hoax by which to extract money from innocent pilgrims. A figure of Christ on the cross, called the Rood of Grace, was made of wood, paste, wire and paper. The monks would hide in a corner of the church and, using a system of pulleys, manipulate the figure so that it moved its head, shook its feet and even changed its facial expressions. It was a sort of sophisticated puppet and must have both amazed and terrified those who saw it. Pilgrims would imagine that they had seen a miracle and leave the monks a hefty donation. Another hoax involved a statue of the child saint St Rumwold. The monks said it could only be lifted from the ground by those who had led a pure life. In fact they had it fixed to the ground by a pin, and if they didn't think you'd given them enough money, they got their revenge by leaving the pin in place. If a pilgrim couldn't lift the statue they were regarded with suspicion by onlookers, and this caused particular stress to female pilgrims, who did not want to gain a reputation for being too free with their affections. The abbey was dissolved in 1538 and the Rood was publicly burned.

Now backtrack along the lanes, past **Boarley Oast** and then turn left, over the new road bridge. Continue uphill towards the Downs, passing **Boarley Farm** on the left. The path now rises steadily to a muddy track. Turn left here along the **Pilgrims' Way** for 300yds (274m). Various paths lead up the escarpment to the right. Go up here into the woods and pick your way through the trees up to the summit. When you reach the **North Downs Way** turn right and follow it through the top of the woods. At two timber hurdles follow the path ahead and then go right to **Harp Farm**. Cross **Harp Farm Road** and follow the North Downs Way to the left of a plantation. After 400yds (366m), cross the road ahead, dodging right and left at the lay-by and into **Boxley Wood**.

Continue on the **North Downs Way** to a waymarked post, where you turn right and descend through the woods on the **Centenary Walk** to the **Pilgrims' Way** again. Hop over a couple of stiles and continue going downhill, over another stile, then diagonally right towards **Boxley church**, crossing two more stiles on the way. This brings you back into the village. The poet Alfred, Lord Tennyson (1809–92) lived at **Park House** near here, to be close to his sister. He wrote his poem *The Brook* here, inspired by the local landscape. The poem ends with the famous lines: 'For men may come and men may go, But I go on forever'.

Walk 36

A Dickens of a Walk at Rochester

Rochester's characterful streets are straight out of a Dickens novel.

·DISTANCE·	6 miles (9.7km)
·MINIMUM TIME·	3hrs
·ASCENT / GRADIENT·	98ft (30m) ▲▲ ▲▲
·LEVEL OF DIFFICULTY·	👫 👫 👫
·PATHS·	City streets and footpaths/cycleways
·LANDSCAPE·	Historic townscapes and some rundown riverside sections
·SUGGESTED MAP·	aqua3 OS Explorer 163 Gravesend & Rochester
·START / FINISH·	Grid reference: TQ 746682
·DOG FRIENDLINESS·	Too busy for most dogs
·PARKING·	Blue Boar car park and cathedral car park (fee)
·PUBLIC TOILETS·	At tourist information centre, also at Northgate and Eastgate

BACKGROUND TO THE WALK

In *Our Mutual Friend* (1865), Charles Dickens wrote of 'a ship's hull, with its rusty iron links of cable run out of hawse-holes long discoloured with the iron's rusty tears'. You pass a decaying ship just like this as you walk along the Medway from Rochester to Upnor, and the spirit of Charles Dickens (1812–70) is with you throughout this walk. In the streets of Rochester you'll half expect to meet genial Mr Pickwick coming out of a pub, or see mad Miss Havisham peering from a window still wearing her ancient wedding dress.

Charles Dickens first came to live near Rochester in 1816 as a 'queer small boy' of five, and the area held a fascination for him throughout his life, inspiring much of his work. Wherever you go today you pass places that featured in his novels. There's Eastgate House, which appears as Westgate House in *The Pickwick Papers* (1836–37); Rochester Cathedral, the focal point of his last, unfinished novel, *The Mystery of Edwin Drood* (1870); and Restoration House, which became Satis House in *Great Expectations* (1861), the mysterious, cobwebby home of Miss Havisham. Travel a few miles from Rochester to Cooling churchyard and you can see the tiny 'stone lozenges', the children's gravestones that feature in the opening passage of *Great Expectations*.

Self Taught

Dickens' life in Rochester was happy, although he was a delicate child and never enjoyed good health. However, when his family moved to London a few years later, his life changed. His father John, who always lived above his means, fell deeply into debt and was sent to the Marshalsea Debtor's Prison. Dickens had to work in a blacking factory to help support the family, an experience that shamed him and haunted him throughout his life. He went to work at an attorney's office at the age of 15, but was so keen to write that he taught himself shorthand and eventually found work as a journalist. In 1836 his first novel, *The Pickwick Papers*, was published.

His books made him wealthy and in 1856 Dickens bought Gad's Hill Place near Rochester, a house he had dreamed of owning since he was a child. Here he would write, entertain fellow authors like Hans Christian Andersen and Wilkie Collins, and go for long walks beside the desolate Medway marshes, just as he used to do with his father. He loved to work in an ornate Swiss chalet, which he built in his garden. It had been sent to him as a gift by a friend and arrived, IKEA style, flat packed in boxes – you can imagine the fun he must have had assembling it. The chalet has now been moved and is in the centre of Rochester, by Eastgate House. Dickens died at Gad's Hill in 1870.

Walk 36

Walk 36 Directions

① From the Park-and-Ride point go right into the pedestrianised part of the **High Street**. Turn left up

Crow Lane, then right by **Restoration House**, following the signs for the **Centenary Walk**. After crossing the small park turn right and walk down the hill to the cathedral.

Walk 36

② Cross the road and turn left round the castle. Pass **Satis House**, then turn right and walk by the **River Medway** until you reach **Rochester Bridge**. Cross the bridge and ,at the traffic-lights, go right along **Canal Road**, which runs under the railway bridge.

③ Walk along the river, pass the **Riverside Tavern** and follow the footpath sign. This brings you out to a new estate where you bear right along a footpath/cycle track, which is part of the **Saxon Shore Way**. Keep walking in the same direction along this track, which is intersected by roads at several points. At one point, pass the rusting hull of a ship that could have come from the pages of a Dickens novel.

> **WHERE TO EAT AND DRINK** ℹ
> There is plenty of choice in Rochester itself, which has several pubs, tea rooms and restaurants. On your way out to Upnor you'll pass the **Riverside Tavern**, which offers food like jacket potatoes, baguettes and burgers, and in Upnor itself, next to the castle, there's the tiny **Tudor Rose** pub offering real ales and home-cooked meals.

④ At a bend in the road the **Saxon Shore Way** bears right, crosses industrial land, and then finally takes you close to the riverbank again. At the river continue walking ahead as far as the entrance to **Upnor Castle**.

> **WHILE YOU'RE THERE** ℹ
> **Rochester Castle** was built by the Normans on the remains of an earlier Roman fort. Its walls are 12ft (3.5m) thick in places. Dickens wanted to be buried in the small graveyard in the castle moat but instead Queen Victoria decreed that he should be buried in Westminster Abbey.

⑤ Turn left along Upnor's tiny, and extremely quaint, **High Street**, and then go to the right. Where a road joins from the left, keep walking ahead to join the footpath that runs to the right of the main road. Follow this to **Lower Upnor**, where you turn right to reach the quay and enjoy great views of the Medway. For even better views, take a short detour up the hill to your left. Prehistoric wild animals once roamed these slopes, as archaeological evidence shows. One of the most interesting discoveries in the area was made in 1911, when a group of Royal Engineers working near Upnor dug up the remains of a mammoth dating back to the last ice age. It was taken to the Natural History Museum in London.

⑥ Retrace your steps back into Rochester. After crossing **Rochester Bridge** walk along the **High Street**, passing sights such as the **Six Poor Travellers' Inn** and the **Dickens Centre**. Continue back to the Park-and-Ride point.

> **WHAT TO LOOK FOR** ℹ
> There's a salty, maritime flavour to the pretty hamlet of **Upnor**. The tiny High Street at Upper Upnor is dominated by the castle, built in the 16th century to protect the English fleet, which was frequently anchored further up the Medway by Rochester Castle. The castle saw no action at all for about 100 years and was taken by surprise when in 1667, the Dutch, then at war with England, sailed right past it. They attacked the fleet, burning several ships and stealing the flagship, before sailing back to Holland. It was a national humiliation.

Joust a Stroll Around Offham

An undemanding walk that starts at Offham's village green, where medieval knights would practise their tournament skills.

•DISTANCE•	4½ miles (7.2km)
•MINIMUM TIME•	2hrs
•ASCENT / GRADIENT•	98ft (30m)
•LEVEL OF DIFFICULTY•	
•PATHS•	Easy woodland and farm paths, though not always well signed, some sections of busy road, 3 stiles
•LANDSCAPE•	Flat agricultural land and woods
•SUGGESTED MAP•	aqua3 OS Explorer 148 Maidstone & the Medway Towns
•START / FINISH•	Grid reference: TQ659574
•DOG FRIENDLINESS•	Keep on lead, particularly busy road. Flat terrain makes it good for older, stiffer dogs
•PARKING•	On-street parking in village
•PUBLIC TOILETS•	None on route

BACKGROUND TO THE WALK

Ever fancied trying your hand at jousting? Well now's your chance. For on the village green at Offham is a quintain, the only one that's still in use in England. A quintain, or tilting post, in case you weren't sure, is a wooden post used by knights practising for jousting tournaments. You know, the sort of thing you see in films where the heroine hands her hanky to her lover then watches tearfully as he gallops off to do battle with the villain who wants to claim her for himself.

The Quintain

The quintain is about 9ft (3m) high with a centrally pivoted, horizontal piece of wood on the top which swings about rather like a weather vane. There's a target board at one end and a dangling wooden truncheon at the other.

The object was to hit the target with your lance, then gallop away quickly before getting a whack on the back of the head with the truncheon. It was an effective way of practising horsemanship and of improving one's accuracy with a lance – though probably best not done when nursing a hangover. The Offham quintain is still used every year in the village's May Day celebrations.

Practice Makes Perfect

Apparently Roman horsemen sometimes trained with quintains, but the practise is most commonly associated with medieval knights. In the 12th century, mock battles or mêlées, were a common form of both entertainment and exercise for young knights and could get quite violent. These mêlées grew in popularity and began to concern the authorities and senior churchmen. Such gatherings of armed men could easily be turned into open rebellion and threaten the stability of the country.

During the 13th and 14th centuries the more formal activity of jousting became popular and gradually took the place of the mêlées. Jousting involved two knights in full armour charging at one another on horseback. The object was to unseat your opponent with your lance. Although jousting took place at tournaments, it was not only a game. In the 14th century competitors could be killed, or captured and then held to ransom as the result of a joust. It wasn't until the end of the 15th century that jousting was practised solely as a sport.

This walk, which is very flat and suitable for people who tend to find going uphill and clambering over stiles difficult, takes you from the village green down to the edge of the woods. At this point you are not far from King's Hill, a new settlement built on the site of West Malling airfield. Pilots from here fought in the Battle of Britain, jousting with planes, rather than lances, as their weapons. You then walk through the wood, on to the road and back to Offham by way of a farm.

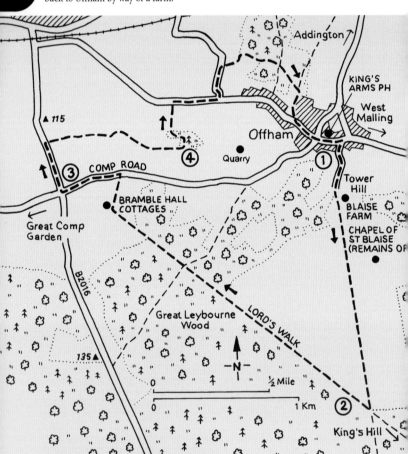

Walk 37 Directions

① With the village green and its distinctive quintain on your right-hand side, walk along the main road and then turn right up **Tower Hill**. Go up the hill to **Blaise Farm** and continue straight ahead, over two stiles. Your route now takes you straight along the track, past the site of a **former chapel** dedicated to

Walk 37

St Blaise – the patron saint of sore throats. He was once said to have miraculously healed a boy who was choking to death on a fishbone. Sadly you can't see any ruins from the footpath – it's hard to imagine that it was ever here. It's an easy stroll now to the edge of the wood (this must be the flattest walk in Kent), where you go sharp right along **Lord's Walk**, which runs along the edge of the wood.

② Join a wide track and keep ahead gradually walking deeper into the woods. Keep ahead until the trees thin and you reach **Bramble Hall Cottages**. Come down to a busy road, then turn left and walk up to a crossroads. The road ahead leads to **Great Comp Garden**, a charming garden surrounding a 17th-century manor. It's one of the less well-known gardens in Kent but is certainly worth a visit.

③ Turn right and walk up the road, take great care as the traffic's very busy. Keep your eyes peeled for a small right of way sign at a gap in the hedge on the right-hand side, opposite a **golf course**. Walk along this track, through a market garden. When you see a hedge ahead of you walk along its left-hand edge. Continue to a typical farm **oast house** and then walk across to a small wood.

④ A stile leads you into the wood and the path goes left, then skirts round the boundary of a quarry. The path brings you out to a main road, where you turn right (take care, it's very busy). After a short distance, cross over and go up the lane on the left. Continue to a footpath on the right. Follow this, crossing over one track, and keep walking ahead to reach a second junction. Turn right and keep ahead, then turn left and return to the **village green**.

Iron Men of Brenchley

This walk from Brenchley takes you back to Kent's industrial past.

•DISTANCE•	4½ miles (7.2km)
•MINIMUM TIME•	2hrs 30min
•ASCENT / GRADIENT•	312ft (95m) ▲▲▲
•LEVEL OF DIFFICULTY•	🚶🚶 🚶🚶 🚶🚶
•PATHS•	Orchard tracks, field margins and footpaths, 14 stiles
•LANDSCAPE•	Varied, rolling landscape of orchards and hop fields
•SUGGESTED MAP•	aqua3 OS Explorer 136 The Weald, Royal Tunbridge Wells
•START / FINISH•	Grid reference: TQ 679418
•DOG FRIENDLINESS•	Good, can run free in many places
•PARKING•	Car park in Brenchley
•PUBLIC TOILETS•	At car park

BACKGROUND TO THE WALK

If you thought there was little more to Kentish history than battles with invaders and the intricacies of apple growing, this walk will soon change your mind. It starts in Brenchley, an atmospheric village with several old timbered houses, a church, pub and – a working forge. The forge, a rare sight these days, is a reminder that Kent once had a thriving iron industry and Brenchley was once at its heart.

The Iron Industry

Even before the Romans came to Britain, iron had been produced in the Weald (the wooded area) of Kent. Ore was extracted from the clay soil and roasted with charcoal (made from the trees) in a small furnace. The resulting molten iron was then hammered into shape. In the 15th and 16th centuries technology improved and large-scale, water-powered blast furnaces and hammer forges were introduced, revolutionising the industry.

Large ponds were created to provide the necessary water power and were given workmanlike names such as Hammer Pond, Pit Pond and, as in the case of the one you pass on this walk, Furnace Pond. The industry grew rapidly and brought prosperity and employment to the Weald – the ironworks at Brenchley once employed 200 men. The industry flourished until the 18th century when it moved to the coal producing regions of the north. Today Furnace Pond is a tranquil place and it's hard to believe that there was once a noisy and bustling ironworks here.

A Revolt for Social Change

A blacksmith called Wat Tyler once lived at Brenchley and gained notoriety by leading the Peasants' Revolt in 1381. This rebellion, which originated from the introduction of a hated poll tax, began in Kent and Essex and soon spread throughout the country. Tyler and his men marched to London, took control of the Tower and murdered various unpopular figures including the Archbishop of Canterbury.

The authorities were unable to take control of the mob and some semblance of calm was only restored when Richard II, then just 14, rode out to meet the rebels. He agreed to meet many of their demands and promised freedom from serfdom (peasants in those days

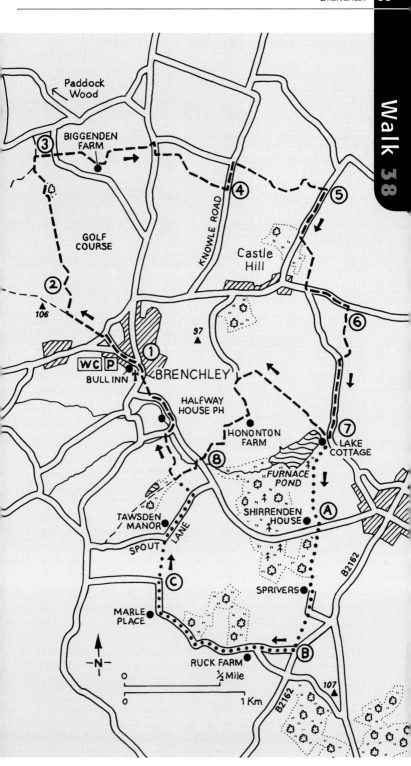

Walk 38

were not free but had to work for the lord of the manor). However, Tyler made further demands and was consequently killed at Smithfield, probably by the Lord Mayor of London. The authorities rapidly regained control and crushed the rebellion. The King went back on his word, serfdom was not abolished and little was gained from so much bloodshed.

Walk 38 Directions

① From the car park turn left to the war memorial. Turn right, then left at the top of the road and go up some steps into an orchard. Walk ahead, crossing two stiles, then turn left to pass some cottages. Continue through the orchard, nip over a stile and on to the **golf course**.

② Pass between the greens on the track, skirting the corner of a wood. Take the track on the right, climb a stile and join the road.

③ Walk a few paces to the right and then climb a stile on your left. Cross the field and follow the track to **Biggenden Farm**, where you cross a stile, turn left and eventually reach the road. Walk to the right and then take the path on the left. Cross a stile and the field beyond, then bear right. Continue towards the tree line and go up steps to **Knowle Road**.

④ Turn left, then, where the road bends, take the path on the right. Head across the field towards the hedge line, maintaining direction to

WHAT TO LOOK FOR

An avenue of **yew trees**, more than 400 years old, dominates the entrance to All Saints Church at Brenchley. Yew trees are a common sight in churchyards and there are many myths and legends attached to them. Some are older than the churches and indicate that the site was once used for pagan worship as yews were considered to be sacred trees.

cross a bridge and a stile. Bear left then right over another bridge and stile, to join the road.

⑤ Turn right past some hop fields, then take a path on the left. Soon turn right through an orchard to a road. Turn left past a pond, then right on a path at a vineyard.

WHERE TO EAT AND DRINK

The **Bull Inn** at Brenchley serves teas, coffees and sandwiches, as well as main meals. The menu features traditional English dishes and Mexican food.

⑥ Continue to a white timbered house, nip over a stile and walk between the gardens to another stile. Turn right to join the main road, then left and up to a parking area at **Furnace Pond**.

⑦ Turn right at **Lake Cottage**, right again across the bridge and walk around the pond. Join the path on the right and walk up the side of an orchard, to turn right at a waymarker. Continue across to a lane. Turn left and walk to **Hononton Farm**. Turn right along the track, through an orchard, then left at a gap in the windbreak. Turn right at the waymarker to the road.

⑧ Cross over, then take the track to your left. Follow this past the house, over a stile and turn right. Cross two more stiles and a bridge. Eventually turn right to join the road at the **Halfway House** pub. Half-way up the hill take the track on your right, cross the field and return to **Brenchley**.

Brenchley's Furnace Pond

This loop takes in two National Trust sites.
See map and information panel for Walk 38

•DISTANCE•	6 miles (9.7km)
•MINIMUM TIME•	3hrs 30min
•ASCENT / GRADIENT•	148ft (45m) ▲▲ ▲ ▲
•LEVEL OF DIFFICULTY•	🚶🚶 🚶🚶 🚶🚶

Walk 39 Directions (Walk 38 option)

From Point ⑦, on Walk 38, take the track on your left before **Lake Cottage** and walk along the side of the cottage fence until you come to a stile. Walk ahead with **Furnace Pond** on your right.

The First World War poet Siegfried Sassoon (1886–1967) was born in Brenchley and he retained a deep love of the surrounding countryside, writing of the 'green contentedness' of the Weald. When he was a child he was taken in a red sledge pulled by ponies, to Furnace Pond when it had frozen over '…my mother drove the sledge across the pond in great style and we felt that we had done something splendid…'.

Go through the wood, then cross a stile and stroll over the open field keeping the wooden fence on your right. After you've crossed a stile at the top of the field, go forward to the hard track past **Shirrenden House** and on to the road, Point Ⓐ.

Cross over and carry on into the woods, eventually passing **Sprivers**, a National Trust garden. Continue ahead to leave the woods and cross into an orchard. Walk between the houses and on to the road, Point Ⓑ.

Turn right on to **Marle Place Road**, walk past **Ruck Farm** and continue past **Marle Place**, another National Trust garden. Carry on to the top of the hill. Where the road swings to the left, join the track that branches off to the right, Point Ⓒ.

Follow this through an orchard (don't worry about the 'no entry' sign, it only applies to vehicles). Turn right at the end on to **Spout Lane** and descend the hill, past **Tawsden Manor**, until you join a footpath going off to the left. Follow this to a wooden bridge over a stream, where you rejoin Walk 38, just after Point ⑧.

WHILE YOU'RE THERE ⓘ
If you like strolling round gardens (and then going home and feeling dissatisfied with your own) then pay a visit to **Marle Place Gardens**. There are 10 acres (4ha) of grounds ranged around the 17th-century house including several different styles of garden. There's a scented garden, a bog garden, a woodland garden and an herbaceous border. You can also see topiary and a restored Victorian greenhouse with a good collection of orchids.

A Ritual Tour of Trottiscliffe

An easy circular walk passing the ancient Coldrum Stones.

•DISTANCE•	4 miles (6.4km)
•MINIMUM TIME•	2hrs
•ASCENT / GRADIENT•	345ft (105m) ▲▲▲
•LEVEL OF DIFFICULTY•	林 林 林
•PATHS•	Easily walked field and woodland paths
•LANDSCAPE•	Ancient landscape of woodland and dramatic downland
•SUGGESTED MAP•	aqua3 OS Explorer 148 Maidstone & the Medway Towns
•START / FINISH•	Grid reference: TQ 642602
•DOG FRIENDLINESS•	Can mostly run free except in parts of Trosley Country Park
•PARKING•	Village hall car park, School Lane
•PUBLIC TOILETS•	Village hall if open

Walk 40 Directions

This walk, which starts at the car park in the village of Trottiscliffe (pronounced Trosley), takes you through a country park high on the North Downs and past an ancient burial site. The village was once the home of the Second World War artist Graham Sutherland (1903–80). Sutherland painted portraits as well as landscapes and these were often controversial, as they tended to be unflattering. He is best remembered for his 80th birthday portrait of Churchill, which Churchill famously detested.

Turn left into **School Lane**, pass the primary school and continue to the T-junction. Turn right up **Taylor's Lane**, go past the **Plough** pub and

---

WHILE YOU'RE THERE ⓘ

Addington, just on the other side of the M20 from Trottiscliffe, is also the site of some ancient burial chambers. Best known is the Chestnuts, a chambered barrow that contained nine cremated bodies and two infants.

---

take the second turning on the right, which is **Green Lane**, a bridleway. You'll see fine examples of Kentish tile hanging and weatherboarding on the cottages to the left. Timber was the most readily available building material until the 17th-century when the forests began to disappear. Timber-framed buildings often look lopsided because builders in Tudor times used fresh, green wood, that twisted as it dried out. Tiles, made of local clay, were often hung on to houses to give extra protection against the elements, particularly during the 17th and 18th centuries when they were very fashionable. Weatherboarding with wood was an alternative to tile hanging.

Pass the allotments on the left and follow the bridleway beside a garden. At the end of the garden your route turns left and heads north through a field with a high hedge to the left. There are good views now of the North Downs escarpment. Go through two sets of kissing gates and you'll see **Trosley Country Park** signed ahead. One of

Walk 40

WHAT TO LOOK FOR

The **North Downs** is a huge chalk escarpment that runs through Kent. Its steep south-facing slope is wooded and is etched with ancient trackways, like the Pilgrims' Way, which have been used for thousands of years.

Kent's first country parks, this was once the estate belonging to Trosley Towers mansion. It covers 160 acres (64.8ha) of the North Downs.

Turn left and continue along the lane to the junction with **Taylor's Lane** and **Vigo Hill**. Turn right and walk diagonally north east to go through a kissing gate marked with a sign stating, rather mysteriously, 'Dogs on lead, sheep not grazing'. You'll know if you've taken the right path if you see a solitary silver birch ahead. Pass through three more kissing gates as you ascend towards the woodland. Continue going up through the wood until you turn right to follow the **North Downs Way**. Keep on this broad path, ignoring offshoots to either side.

Eventually your path bears left uphill and through a kissing gate. Turn right and make your way downhill, continuing to follow the North Downs Way. This is an incredibly atmospheric part of the walk. The lane is deep and the trees form a thick canopy overhead; it feels as if it hasn't changed for thousands of years. At the foot of the woodland cross the **Pilgrims' Way** and join the **Wealdway** to continue your descent through fields down to the **Coldrum Stones**. This is a neolithic burial site dating back to the 3rd millennium BC. Originally there would have been a circle of upright stones on the site, surrounding a large earthen burial chamber. This in turn would have

been divided by large stones, creating interior chambers. This style of construction is similar to that of tombs found in north west Europe, but in Britain is confined to North Kent. It shows that there were close cultural links between the two areas. When the barrow was excavated in 1910, the remains of 22 people were discovered as well as the bones of a deer, an ox, rabbit and fox. There seem to be various theories about the site. The skeletons are said to have physical similarities, so they could belong to members of the same family, buried there perhaps over a number of years. Another theory is that the grave belonged to a chieftain, and that when he died his family (and perhaps his slaves) would have been killed so as to accompany him on his journey to the afterlife.

To return to the village you can either backtrack and follow the waymarks left through the fields, or continue downhill from the barrow on the concrete track and on to the lane. Either way brings you to the junction of **Pinesfield Lane** and **Church Lane**, with the Church of St Peter and St Paul on the right. This is of Norman origin and boasts a large pulpit that came from Westminster Abbey. Just by the church is a picturesque cluster of buildings that once surrounded a palace of the Bishops of Rochester. Return to the village from the fingerpost in front of the church, either by following the footpath bearing left or by the bridleway straight ahead.

WHERE TO EAT AND DRINK

There are two pubs where you can eat in Trottiscliffe, the **George** and the **Plough**. Both have beer gardens and serve bar meals and snacks.

3/8/08   Aud, Phyl, Hazel, Ann
+ me

Tasting the Waters at Tunbridge Wells

A simple trail through this elegant spa town, discovering the origins of its famous Pantiles and Royal patronage.

•DISTANCE•	3 miles (4.8km)
•MINIMUM TIME•	1hr 30min
•ASCENT / GRADIENT•	197ft (60m) ▲▲▲
•LEVEL OF DIFFICULTY•	🚶🚶 🚶🚶 🚶🚶
•PATHS•	Paved streets and tarmac paths
•LANDSCAPE•	Bustling town and leafy common
•SUGGESTED MAP•	aqua3 OS Explorer 147 Sevenoaks & Tonbridge
•START / FINISH•	Grid reference: TQ 582388
•DOG FRIENDLINESS•	They'll like common and rocks, otherwise it's a bit too busy
•PARKING•	Car park behind The Pantiles
•PUBLIC TOILETS•	Tunbridge Wells centre

BACKGROUND TO THE WALK

As you walk through the elegant streets of Tunbridge Wells, you quickly become aware that there are no medieval or Tudor buildings at all. This is because, until the 17th-century, there was nothing here except thick woodland and areas of common. The town only grew up after Dudley, Lord North, whose health had been suffering from too much high living, discovered a spring while out riding in 1606. He noticed that the waters were brown and looked similar to those at a spa in Belgium. He took a drink and soon felt better (possibly feeling that if it tastes that bad it must be good for you). Word quickly spread and the great and the good started to come here to taste the waters for themselves.

Royal Patronage

The area became very popular, as it was much closer to London than other spa towns like Bath or Buxton and it soon attracted a royal visitor, Queen Henrietta Maria, Charles I's wife. As there was nowhere to stay, she and her entourage had to camp out on the common. Later visitors included Charles II, who brought both his wife and Nell Gwynne (though not necessarily at the same time), Samuel Pepys, Beau Nash and Daniel Defoe.

Gradually, lodging houses grew up around the spring, which was enclosed in the Bath House so that people could take warm, curative baths as well as drink the waters. The area around the spring was laid out into 'walks' where people could promenade – for this was now the place to see and to be seen. The 'season' ran from Easter to October, when the roads from London were passable.

The Pantiles

When Queen Anne's son fell on the slippery ground she gave the town £100 so the walk could be paved with clay tiles known as pantiles. When she came back a year later she was furious to find that nothing had been done and created a regal rumpus – leading some to suggest that she was the original 'Disgusted of Tunbridge Wells'. Eventually the work was carried out and The Pantiles, which you reach at the end of this walk, are still the heart of the town and have retained their elegance. Today Tunbridge Wells, which was given the right to be called 'Royal' in 1909, is the sort of place where you come to stroll, shop, browse in bookshops and have tea and cakes while watching the world go by. Apart from the traffic it feels as if very little has changed since the town's heyday in the 17th and 18th centuries.

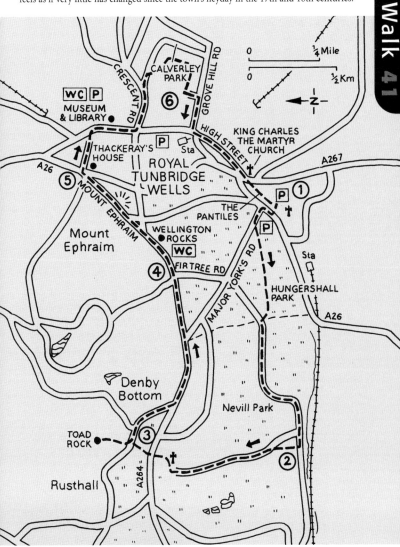

Walk 41 Directions

① From the car park behind The Pantiles, turn right and walk up to the main road. Cross over, and then walk up **Major York's Road**. Just

after the car park take the footpath to the left and walk across the common, keeping ahead until you reach **Hungershall Park**, where you turn left. Keep following the road until you come to a footpath that leads up to the right.

② Follow this path up through the trees which eventually leads on to a private road. Continue walking ahead and when you reach the top take the track that runs ahead through the trees. After a horse barrier, bear right to pass the churchyard, then turn right and walk around the **church** and up to the busy main road.

> **WHILE YOU'RE THERE** ℹ
>
> If you come to Tunbridge Wells during the summer you'll be able to try the waters of the **Chalybeate Spring** that Lord North discovered. Their taste comes from the high iron content – 'chalybeate' is derived from the Greek word for iron. The water also contains many minerals and is said to help conditions such as arthritis and anaemia. They also say that it's good for hangovers.

③ Turn right, then cross to walk up to the turning on the left signed '**Toad Rock**'. The path now winds uphill to the rock (it does look rather like a toad, doesn't it?). Now return to the main road and turn left. Continue until you pass **Fir Tree Road**. On the common, hidden by the trees, are **Wellington Rocks**. If you've got a dog with you, this is a good place for them to have a run.

④ Continue along **Mount Ephraim** to some cottages on the right that are built into the rock. There are seats here and you get good views over the town. Turn right to walk across the grass to the picturesque

> **WHERE TO EAT AND DRINK** ℹ
>
> There are plenty of places to choose from but my favourite is the **Regency Restaurant and Tea Rooms**, which is situated on The Pantiles. The tea is good and they serve enormous slices of traditional sponge cakes, as well as scones and light meals. You can sit outside if the weather's good.

old house that was once home to the author William Makepeace Thackeray (it's, unsurprisingly, known as **Thackeray's House**).

⑤ Go along the path that runs by the left of the house and walk along **Mount Ephraim Road**. This brings you out in front of a pedestrianised shopping area. Turn right and walk down, past the museum and library and the war memorial. Turn left to walk up **Crescent Road** and continue until you reach **Calverley Park**, a 19th-century housing development designed by Decimus Burton. As you enter the park you'll see an oak tree planted in honour of Air Chief Marshall Lord Dowding who once lived here.

⑥ Walk across **Calverley Grounds** to go down **The Mews**, then go right into **Grove Hill Road**. This brings you down to a roundabout where you turn left and walk along the **High Street**. At the end go down **Chapel Place**, pass the Church of King Charles the Martyr, cross the road and then walk along the famous **Pantiles** and back to the car park.

> **WHAT TO LOOK FOR** ℹ
>
> On this walk you'll pass two **sandstone outcrops**, a distinctive feature of the area. Many of these outcrops have unusual shapes and became popular visitor attractions during Victorian times. Toad Rock was once described as the local equivalent of the Leaning Tower of Pisa. The rocks made convenient shelters for the mesolithic hunters who lived in the Weald and archaeological evidence has shown that they used to camp beneath them. Today the rocks are home to rare mosses, ferns and liverworts.

History and Mystery at Ightham Mote

An easy walk to one of Kent's moated manor houses, probably one of the best examples of its kind in the country.

Walk 42

•**DISTANCE**•	3½ miles (5.7km)
•**MINIMUM TIME**•	1hr 30min
•**ASCENT / GRADIENT**•	98ft (30m) ▲ ▲ ▲
•**LEVEL OF DIFFICULTY**•	🚶 🚶 🚶
•**PATHS**•	Easily walked fields and estate paths, short sections on roads, can be muddy in places, 8 stiles
•**LANDSCAPE**•	Well-maintained historic parkland and fertile pasture
•**SUGGESTED MAP**•	aqua3 OS Explorer 147 Sevenoaks & Tonbridge
•**START / FINISH**•	Grid reference: TQ 592524
•**DOG FRIENDLINESS**•	Livestock in some fields and on estate, but still enjoyable for most dogs
•**PARKING**•	Chaser Inn car park – ask landlord's permission
•**PUBLIC TOILETS**•	None on route

BACKGROUND TO THE WALK

Unlike other counties in England, Kent has few grand stately homes and large estates, but is instead liberally scattered with attractive farmsteads and manor houses which give the landscape a lovely patchwork effect and add enormous variety to local walks. Yet it is only like this because, after the Norman Conquest, the people of Kent (who had a reputation for being independent and a bit aggressive) offered allegiance to William on condition that he allowed them to retain their Saxon traditions and privileges. In return they agreed to give him Dover Castle without a fight. William agreed and for centuries Kent continued to operate under its traditional administrative system. One of those traditions concerned inheritance, which in Kent followed the Jutish law of gavelkind. This meant that property and land would be split equally between a man's sons – rather than simply being passed to the eldest. So the land was divided into small, self-sufficient units.

A Hidden Treasure

Ightham Mote, which you pass on this walk, is typical of the county – a moated medieval manor house deep in the countryside, yet full of local history. The house is some distance from the village of Ightham and so well hidden that it comes as something of a surprise when you find it. Apparently, during the Civil War Cromwell's soldiers set off to loot the house but lost their way in the tangle of country lanes (Kent's signposting obviously wasn't up to much then either) and raided another house by mistake.

Despite its name, the term 'mote' is more likely to refer to the fact that the house was built on an ancient meeting place, or 'mot', than to the medieval moat that surrounds it. For hundreds of years the house was owned by the Selby family, whose most famous member was Dame Dorothy Selby. There's a rather cryptic memorial to her in the local church that mentions that she 'disclos'd the Plot'; seeming to imply that she foiled the Gunpowder Plot in 1605. Legend has it that she wrote an anonymous letter to her cousin, Lord Mounteagle, warning him to stay away from the opening of Parliament. He was said to have been disturbed by this and made investigations, which led to the discovery of Guy Fawkes. However, it seems more likely that Dame Dorothy, a skilled needlewoman, had simply embroidered a rather vivid picture of the Plot that people admired and remembered.

Early in the 19th century Ightham Mote was let to an American general, William Jackson Palmer. He loved entertaining and during his time there many contemporary celebrities, including the painters Edward Burne-Jones and John Singer Sargent, the novelist Henry James and the craftsman William Morris, visited the house.

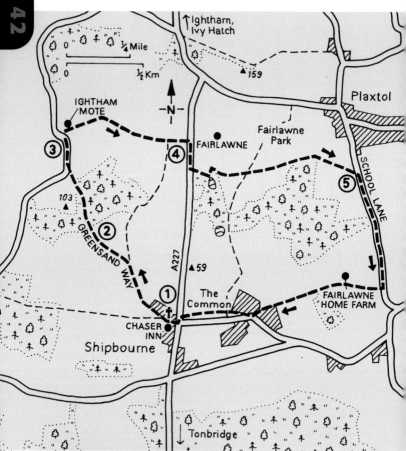

Walk 42 **Directions**

① From the **Chaser Inn** walk to your left, through the church lychgate, following the signs for the **Greensand Way**. Walk to the right-hand side of the church, go through a little gate, then over the stile on the right. Cross the field to another stile and follow the **Greensand Way** signs, walking across a field to another stile. Go a few paces to the right, then straight ahead, walking up through another field.

② Half-way across this field there is a footpath sign by an oak tree.

Walk 42

Follow this, then cross another stile and go into the woods along a fenced path. Another stile leads you out of the woods, where you turn right and walk around the edge of a field. Hop over a stile, then turn right into the lane and up to the entrance to **Ightham Mote**.

③ Go through the entrance and walk straight ahead, keeping the manor house to your left. Keep walking straight ahead, go over a stile and follow the footpath signed 'A227'. Go across a field to a stile and turn right on to the **A227**.

④ Walk along the road, then cross over at the entrance to the **Fairlawne Estate**. This was once the home of Sir Harry Vane, who, although a Parliamentary sympathiser, was so unpopular with Cromwell that he had him imprisoned. Harry was even more unpopular with Charles II who had him beheaded on Tower Hill. Needless to say, Sir Harry is said to haunt the grounds of Fairlawne. Go into the estate and then take the right-hand fork that leads to a pond. Go through a white gate (marked 'private no entry') and walk across the estate, down a pleasant tree-lined walk and out on to **School Lane**.

⑤ Turn right and walk along the road until you see the sign on the right-hand side for **Fairlawne Home Farm**, where you join the **Greensand Way**. Walk along the track until you come out on to the common. Bear right and you will see tennis courts ahead of you. Keep the tennis courts on your right and walk across the common, soon to come down to **Shipbourne church** and the **Chaser Inn**.

Walk 43

Hadlow's Folly

This walk starts from a village dominated by an extraordinary folly.

•DISTANCE•	4 miles (6.4km)
•MINIMUM TIME•	2hrs
•ASCENT / GRADIENT•	262ft (80m) ▲▲▲
•LEVEL OF DIFFICULTY•	🚶🚶 🚶🚶 🚶🚶
•PATHS•	Field edges, woodland tracks, some road, 15 stiles
•LANDSCAPE•	Pleasant views over the Weald, and lots of oast houses
•SUGGESTED MAP•	aqua3 OS Explorer 148 Maidstone & the Medway Towns
•START / FINISH•	Grid reference: TQ 644526
•DOG FRIENDLINESS•	Lots of stiles but several sections off lead
•PARKING•	On-street parking in Hadlow.
•PUBLIC TOILETS•	Court Lane, Hadlow

BACKGROUND TO THE WALK

One feature dominates the landscape on this walk and you'll see it as soon as you arrive in the village. It's the enormous tower built in the early 19th century by local eccentric Walter Barton May as an extension to Hadlow Castle. It's not particularly decorative – it could be mistaken for a functional water tower – but it is one of the largest and most interesting follies in Britain.

The name 'folly' comes from the French word for foolishness. An appropriate term, as it's applied to eye-catching, expensive, largely useless buildings that were built to enhance the landscape. They were very fashionable in the 18th and early 19th centuries and were a 'must-have' for wealthy landowners, who would construct them in the landscaped grounds surrounding their mansions. Favourite designs were classical temples and ruined castles, which often had ivy trained up them just to add a touch of realism. One of the best-known of the landscaped gardens that were filled with follies is Stourhead in Wiltshire.

The folly at Hadlow looks as if it is made of stone, but it is in fact a brick structure covered by stucco – a technique commonly used in the 19th century by those who couldn't afford genuine stone. If you look closely you can see the stucco peeling off.

As follies go, May's isn't the most unusual in Britain; that honour surely has to go to the giant Pineapple folly in Dunmore Park near Airth in Scotland. However, it is one of the most mysterious. Some people claim that May built the tower so that he could get a view of the sea – which seems highly unlikely from this part of Kent. Others claim that it was a copy of another tower at Fonthill Abbey in Wiltshire and was the final stage in the construction of his home, Hadlow Castle. However, the most widely believed, and certainly most interesting, theory is that May built it so that he could spy on his wife who was having a fling with a local farmer. His wife certainly left him, although not until after the tower was finished, so May was stuck with a prominent reminder of her infidelity.

If you go into the churchyard you can see the elaborate mausoleum belonging to this eccentric man. He ordered it specially because he wanted to be buried sitting up, above the ground – perhaps because he wanted to be able to watch what was going on in the graveyard. Sadly, but perhaps unsurprisingly, May's wishes weren't carried out and he was buried lying down.

Old Soar Manor

(C) Hurst Wood

▲ 165

(A)

(B)

YOTES COURT

HURST FOLLY

STAN LANE

West Peckham

FORGE LANE

Mereworth

WEALDWAY

(4)

DUKES PLACE

GREENSAND WAY

Court Lodge Farm

SWAN PH

(5)

OXEN HOATH

WEALDWAY

Hazel Wood

Oxen Hoath Park

The Common

▲ 35

GOOSE GREEN FARM

A26

(6)

Goose Green

(3)

—N—

0   ¼ Mile

0   ½ Km

FIDDLING MONKEY PH

(1)

HADLOW CASTLE

HADLOW

GOBLANDS FARM

(2)

Tonbridge

Walk 43 **Directions**

① From the centre of the village walk north past the **Fiddling Monkey** pub. Follow the public footpath sign on the right, walk across a field and take the left-hand field edge. Cross a stile and walk ahead across an orchard. Cross another stile and you will see **Goblands Farm** in front of you.

② Turn left, then take the footpath on the right, over a little bridge and into a field. Turn left and walk round the field, then cross a stile on the left, followed by a tiny bridge. Go straight ahead and cross another field walking in the direction of an **oast house**. Cross a stile and another small bridge and walk across the next field to a stile. Continue in this direction over two more stiles, then go through a garden and on to the lane.

WHAT TO LOOK FOR ⓘ
The church in West Peckham is Saxon in origin and well worth a look if it's open when you pass. Inside is a **Squires Pew**, which has its own separate entrance. It's very comfortable and offers complete privacy – not only from the congregation, but from the vicar too.

③ Turn left, cross the main road and go through the gate of **Goose Green Farm**. Follow the driveway, then turn right through a gap in a fence and follow the footpath across a field. On reaching some woodland take the path that runs to the left, through the wood. Walk up to the farm and into the little village of **West Peckham**.

④ Walk across the village green to the top left-hand corner. Go through a kissing gate and follow the signs for the **Greensand Way**. Follow the track and go round to the right of a cottage and over a stile. Walk around the edge of a field to another stile. At a road, go left for a few paces, then right along the track. Follow the edge of a field then cross another stile.

WHILE YOU'RE THERE ⓘ
The nearby village of **Mereworth** serves as an interesting reminder of the power that wealthy landowners once wielded. When the mansion house was built there in the 18th century, the owner decided that the village rather spoiled his view – so he built a new village and had the old one demolished.

⑤ Where the **Wealdway** goes right, turn left and walk down to the gates of **Oxen Hoath**. Walk past the house, cross a cattle grid and walk ahead keeping the pond on your left. Cross a stile, walk across fields to another stile, and then hop over a third stile and on to the road.

⑥ Cross the road, walk along the tarmac then turn left, signposted for the common. Just before you reach some cottages take the lane on the right. Follow this, cross a stile and then turn left and walk round the edge of a field. Cross two more stiles and go through a kissing gate on to the road. Turn right and walk back into the village.

WHERE TO EAT AND DRINK ⓘ
Grays Tea House is an immaculate little tea room on the main street in Hadlow. The tea is served in proper china pots and the cakes are fresh and home-made. You can have snacks and light meals as well. The **Swan** on the green in West Peckham has a good reputation for its food and welcomes children and dogs. They brew their own beer and serve snacks as well as full meals.

A Walk from West Peckham

A longer, more energetic walk through woodlands.
See map and information panel for Walk 43

·DISTANCE·	6 miles (9.7km)
·MINIMUM TIME·	3hrs
·ASCENT / GRADIENT·	541ft (165m) ▲▲▲
·LEVEL OF DIFFICULTY·	🚶 🚶 🚶

Walk 44 Directions (Walk 43 option)

Leave Walk 43, in West Peckham, at Point ④. Turn right at the church, which can trace its origins back to Saxon times, and walk up to a junction. If you've got time, continue ahead for a short distance to a house known as **Dukes Place**, which was believed
to have had associations with the Knights Templars who once owned land here. The Templars were an order of Christian knights established during the crusades in the 12th century to protect pilgrims travelling to the Holy Land. They became immensely powerful and rather mysterious.

Turn left up **Forge Lane**, then right up **Stan Lane** which runs to the right of **Old Forge Cottage**. Walk up the hill and turn right along the bridleway at **Hurst Folly**, Point ④.

Walk through woodland, then head downhill to a cottage. Walk to the left of this and descend to **Yotes Court**. Don't be tempted to go right, down into the farmyard, or down the well-marked path to the left of it. Instead keep a sharp eye out for an unmarked lane on your immediate left, Point Ⓑ.

Walk along the lane, across fields and over a stile. After crossing the stile turn left and then turn right, opposite an entrance to a house. Walk past a pond, then pass some cottages on the left-hand side. When you reach a wood cross the road and walk up a bridle path through the wood.

At the first distinct cross paths, Point Ⓒ, go left and walk down, crossing over a metalled track. Continue in the same direction to a road and turn right. Soon come to a junction and follow the **Wealdway** until it bears hard left. Now rejoin the Walk 43 at Point ⑤.

WHILE YOU'RE THERE ⓘ

At **Old Soar Manor** at Plaxtol, not far from Hadlow, you can see the remains of a 13th-century knight's house with its private quarters and chapel. There's a Georgian house on the site of the old manor hall. They say that a young servant girl, Jenny, who was raped by the family priest, haunts the house. When she realised she was pregnant she asked the local parson what she should do. He told her to marry the father. The girl fainted at the thought, fell and drowned in the font. When she was found it was believed she had committed suicide and she was buried in unconsecrated ground.

Roman Round Eynsford

This easy and enjoyable walk takes you past a preserved Roman villa.

•DISTANCE•	5 miles (8km)
•MINIMUM TIME•	2hrs
•ASCENT / GRADIENT•	197ft (60m) ▲▲▲
•LEVEL OF DIFFICULTY•	🏃🏃 🏃🏃 🏃
•PATHS•	Woodland, riverside and field paths, mostly firm underfoot
•LANDSCAPE•	River valley and rolling parkland
•SUGGESTED MAP•	aqua3 OS Explorers 147 Sevenoaks & Tonbridge; 162 Greenwich & Gravesend
•START / FINISH•	Grid reference: TQ 540655 (on Explorer 162)
•DOG FRIENDLINESS•	Great, several sections where they can run free. Popular local dog walking route
•PARKING•	Car park in Eynsford
•PUBLIC TOILETS•	At car park

Walk 45 Directions

This walk takes you into the heart of the Darent Valley, an area that has been settled for thousands of years. Although close to London, the area still retains a rural feel and and offers glorious views over the surrounding countryside.

From the car park by the post office on Eynsford's main street, turn right to walk down **Riverside**, the road opposite the **church**. Go over the bridge by the ford from which the village takes its name. This has been an important crossing point on the Darent since Roman times. Walk up past the **Plough Inn**, then

> **WHILE YOU'RE THERE** ⓘ
> **Eynsford Castle** was built by the Normans and was originally surrounded by a moat but was more of a fortified house than a defensive structure. It was destroyed by fire in the 13th century and today you can see the remains of its walls and part of the empty moat.

past **Sparepenny Lane**. You'll often see this name on country lanes. It dates back to the days when you had to pay a toll if you wanted to travel on a turnpike road. Sparepenny Lane would probably have been a private road that was cheaper than the main turnpike.

At the last house on the right, bear right and go through a gate into a field. Cut across this to cross a stile at the top, then walk – carefully – across the railway line. Pop over another stile then walk straight across the next field to go through a gap in the fence. Cross the lane and follow the path across the next field, taking time to enjoy some great views across the valley. When you reach the post at the top, go to the right of the hedge, then walk ahead keeping the hedge on your left-hand side. Cross a stile, turn right up the enclosed path and where it bends go left, through a gap in the hedge. Your path now continues across the top of a field, dips slightly, then takes you between

Walk 45

some trees, where you'll see part of a golf course on your left. Where the path forks, go left through a horse barrier and up some steps into the woods. Come out of the woods after another barrier, go a few paces right, then left again to continue over the top of the field. Turn left to go through another barrier, go back into the woods and walk ahead, keeping the **golf course** on your left. Reach a broad track, go a few paces left then continue ahead, keeping the fairways to either side of you. Soon reach a tarmac track, turn right and walk up towards the clubhouse.

At the wooden fingerpost turn left and walk across the fairway to go down into the woods (take care you don't get hit by a golf ball here). Walk ahead until you come to a metal fence and turn left. Pass a ladder stile on your right-hand side and keep walking ahead, following the signs to the visitor centre. Maintain your direction until you see a marker post. Turn right here, go through a barrier and walk downhill to the visitor centre. There are lovely views on the way down of **Eynsford Viaduct**, an elegant red brick structure built for the railway in the 19th century.

Your route now goes past the visitor centre, then bears left just before the road, along the **Darent Valley Path**. Your walk takes on a restful quality along the banks of the

> ### WHAT TO LOOK FOR ⓘ
> I saw a couple of **green woodpeckers** last time I did this walk. They'd given their presence away by their distinctive tapping sound. Woodpeckers don't only make their nests in the trunks of trees but also feed on insects that they find in the bark. They have very long tongues that allow them to seek them out.

Darent. There is a good chance of seeing dragonflies, coots and moorhens along here – if it's quiet you could even catch a glimpse of a kingfisher. Plants that grow in the river include water crowfoot, while meadowsweet, marsh marigolds and willow trees line its banks.

Keep walking by the river until you pass the lake and weir and emerge by the entrance of **Lullingstone Castle**. This is a Tudor manor house, dating back to the reign of Henry VIII, with an 18th-century façade. Lullingstone frequently played host to royal visitors, including Queen Anne, for whom an outdoor bathhouse was built. Walk past the gateway of the castle and along the road to the green corrugated iron shed that protects the remains of Lullingstone Roman Villa. Built in the 1st century AD on the site of an Iron-Age farm, this superbly preserved villa was built by Roman settlers and occupied by several different families. You can see the bathhouse, exquisite mosaic flooring and the system of under floor heating. Worth looking out for is the paw print of a small dog, embedded in a tile which had just been made. Keep the villa on your left and walk straight ahead, past signs for a bird of prey centre, and underneath the viaduct. Your way now takes you close to the River Darent again and back, over the ford, into **Eynsford**.

> ### WHERE TO EAT AND DRINK ⓘ
> You've got plenty of choice along this route. There's a tea room at **Lullingstone Park Visitor Centre** and several picnic tables outside. In Eynsford there's the **Plough Inn**, a large, modernised pub by the riverside, and the more traditional **Malt Shovel**.

Walk 46

Churchill's Hideaway at Westerham

This lovely walk across thickly wooded commons takes you to Chartwell, Winston Churchill's historic home.

•DISTANCE•	5 miles (8km)
•MINIMUM TIME•	2hrs
•ASCENT / GRADIENT•	300ft (90m) ▲ ▲ ▲
•LEVEL OF DIFFICULTY•	🚶 🚶 🚶
•PATHS•	Mainly well-signposted woodland paths and bridleways, can be very muddy, short sections on roads, 7 stiles
•LANDSCAPE•	Well-wooded commons and some meadows, excellent on crisp autumn days
•SUGGESTED MAP•	aqua3 OS Explorer 147 Sevenoaks & Tonbridge
•START / FINISH•	Grid reference: TQ 540447
•DOG FRIENDLINESS•	Some sections on lead. Likely to see horses and grazing animals. Loads of woodland smells to investigate
•PARKING•	Car park or on-street parking in Westerham village centre
•PUBLIC TOILETS•	At car park

BACKGROUND TO THE WALK

It might be right in the heart of the Kentish commuter belt, but there's something timeless and deliciously rural about Westerham. It would be easy to imagine that the village has slept peacefully for centuries, undisturbed by the outside world. But during the Second World War, fighter aeroplanes frequently darkened the skies above Westerham, as pilots from nearby Biggin Hill airfield battled overhead to save Britain from invasion.

Home to a Great Statesman

By coincidence, Winston Churchill's country retreat was in Westerham and this walk takes you right past the entrance. Churchill (1874–1965) bought Chartwell in 1922 after losing his parliamentary seat, and at a time when many thought that his political career was over. The house, which required extensive renovation, offered outstanding views over the Weald of Kent. By the time Churchill was re-elected in 1924, Chartwell was the family home.

The house was run on a lavish scale, the staff included eight or nine indoor servants, three gardeners and a chauffeur. When Churchill was made Chancellor of the Exchequer in 1924 his official residence was in Downing Street. However, he would return to Chartwell at weekends and would dictate budget proposals in his bath, 'wallowing, gurgling, turning the taps on and off with his toes, and surfacing with a noise like a whale blowing'.

Work and Play

In 1929 the Conservative government lost power and once again it looked as if Churchill's career was over. He turned his energies to writing (he had always been a prolific author) and would work for hours in his study. His daily routine at Chartwell was a fascinating mixture of hard work and hedonism. He wouldn't get up until about 11AM, preferring to dictate letters and articles to his secretaries while still in bed. After bathing, he'd walk in the garden before going to his study to work until lunch – which would usually be a grand affair with champagne, brandy and cigars. Churchill would return to his study for a few hours, before going back to bed at 5PM for a nap. After dinner, (distinguished guests included Charlie Chaplin and T E Lawrence – who sat at the table dressed as an Arabian warlord) he would return to his study and work into the early hours, sometimes dictating a phenomenal 3,000 words in one session.

When war was declared, Churchill was again offered a ministerial position and in 1940 he was made Prime Minister. Chartwell was closed for the duration of the war, but once it was over Churchill returned to the house and spent his last years here, writing in the study, painting and pottering in the garden.

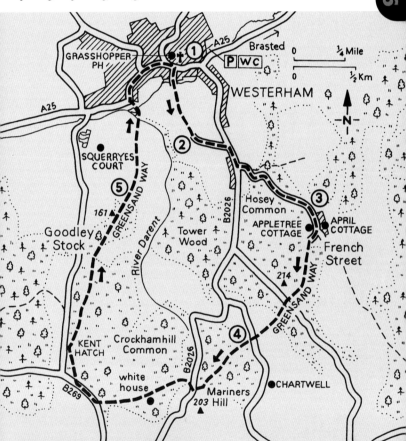

Walk 46 Directions

① From the church in Westerham, walk up to the **village green**, then cross over and head up **Water Lane** opposite the statue of Churchill. Go over a little stone stile, through a gate and straight ahead across the meadow. Continue into a second meadow and, about half-way across, turn left and go through a kissing gate that is well hidden in the hedge.

② Walk down a narrow lane to a road, turn right and continue to a patch of common on the left-hand side. Turn up a metalled lane that runs to the left of a house and through the trees. Soon come to a hard track. Turn right here and follow it to **French Street**.

③ Walk past **April Cottage** and **Appletree Cottage** (which are as pretty as they sound) then follow the bridleway that veers to the right. Where it branches take the left hand track, then follow the **Greensand Way** as it winds through the woods, crossing a minor road. Eventually cross a stile on to another road, the entrance to **Chartwell** is on your immediate left.

④ Cross the road, go up some steps and follow the **Greensand Way** again. Eventually it bears to the right and comes to a main road, **Mariners Hill**. Cross over and

> ### WHERE TO EAT AND DRINK ℹ️
> There's plenty of choice in Westerham. The oldest pub is the **Grasshopper**, originally built to house the masons who built the village church in the 13th century. It later became a coaching inn. Traditional tea shops are **Tiffins** and the **Tudor Rose**, both on the green, and there are several contemporary coffee shops too. The **White Hart** in nearby Brasted was a favourite haunt with Battle of Britain pilots and the pub is full of evocative memorabilia.

> ### WHAT TO LOOK FOR ℹ️
> Part of Hosey Common near Westerham is a nationally important **bat reserve**. Five species of bat live here: Daubenton's, Brandt's, whiskered, Natterer's and brown long-eared. It is unusual to see bats while walking during the day, but you might spot them at dusk – and no, they won't get tangled in your hair; their sonar system (a bit like radar) is far too sophisticated for that.

follow the **Greensand Way** – take care not to slip, as it can be muddy. Follow the path round to the left and up to a very old brick house, called 'The Warren'. Now follow the tarmac track downhill and keep going to another, busier road. Turn right and walk along the road, then turn right again at the small sign for **Kent Hatch**. Walk along the bridleway, past an isolated house dated 1787, and take the track that forks to the left. Go over a stile, passing a 'Toll Riding Route' sign, and follow the **Greensand Way** again.

[handwritten margin note: No sign for KH]

⑤ Eventually the landscape opens out. Cross a stile, and then keep going straight ahead over two more stiles. There are lovely views of **Westerham** ahead. Hop over another stile and follow the path down, past a pool and over a final stile, where you turn left and come into the village. Turn right and walk up the main street to the starting point.

> ### WHILE YOU'RE THERE ℹ️
> **Squerryes Court** is the gorgeous 17th-century manor house you can see as you're making your way back into Westerham, and it is well worth a visit. Unlike many great houses, it is not a museum but a home, belonging to the Warde family who have owned it for generations. The art collection includes works by George Stubbs, Poussin, Rubens and Van Dyck and there's plenty of fine furniture and china. It's impressive but not overwhelming, and you feel as if you could live here quite happily.

Through Parkland at Penshurst

A fairly easy circular walk around the magnificent estate surrounding medieval Penshurst Place.

Walk 47

•DISTANCE•	3½ miles (5.7km)
•MINIMUM TIME•	1hr 45min
•ASCENT / GRADIENT•	148ft (45m) ▲ ▲ ▲
•LEVEL OF DIFFICULTY•	🚶 🚶 🚶
•PATHS•	Broad tracks, short section on busy road, one badly signposted section by river, 2 stiles
•LANDSCAPE•	Leafy parkland with views of Penshurst Place
•SUGGESTED MAP•	aqua3 OS Explorer 147 Sevenoaks & Tonbridge
•START / FINISH•	Grid reference: TQ 527438
•DOG FRIENDLINESS•	Good, although on lead, some dogs might not like unusual squeeze gates
•PARKING•	On-street parking in village, also car park for Penshurst Place
•PUBLIC TOILETS•	Penshurst Road

BACKGROUND TO THE WALK

From the very start of this walk you are rewarded with wonderful views of Penshurst Place, one of the finest medieval manor houses in England. Your route takes you through the lush surrounding parkland, down an avenue of mature trees, then along the grassy banks of the Medway, before you finally pass the house once again.

A Medieval Manor House

Penshurst Place is not just an extremely handsome building, it is also steepd in history. Built in the 14th century, the house has been home to many of England's most notable and colourful characters. They include Humphrey, Duke of Gloucester (1391–1447) and brother of Henry V, who founded the Bodleian Library at Oxford; Edward Stafford, 3rd Duke of Buckingham (1478–1521), who was beheaded by Henry VIII – who then took Penshurst Place for himself; Sir William Sidney (1482–1554), who distinguished himself in battle at Flodden Field and was gifted the property by Edward VI, and his descendent Algernon Sidney (c1622–1683), a republican and supporter of Oliver Cromwell. At the Restoration Algernon was abroad and, feeling it was unsafe to return to live in England, travelled throughout Europe for many years. He eventually returned to Penshurst in order to see his dying father, but unfortunately he was still a marked man and was eventually arrested on trumped up charges by Charles II and beheaded.

Local Hero

Most notable of all these residents was Sir Philip Sidney who was born here in 1554. A poet, soldier and statesman he was one of those people who seemed to do everything well. He was gifted at languages, well read, athletic, a good dancer, witty, handsome, popular – an all round good egg. He was also, for a time, Elizabeth I's favourite courtier and she was reputedly so fond of him that she refused to let him sail to America with Sir Francis Drake – in whose work Sidney was very interested. His poetry was inspired by unrequited love – he was forbidden to marry the woman he really loved – and by the beautiful countryside around Penshurst.

Heroic Loss

However, like many idols, it was only after his death that Sir Philip Sidney was established as an heroic figure. He was badly wounded fighting the Spanish and was brought some water to relieve his thirst. But he saw another wounded soldier being carried past and gave it to him instead saying 'thy necessity is yet greater than mine'. Sidney died a few weeks later aged 32. His loss was felt so greatly that for months it was considered improper to appear at Court, or in the City, in light coloured clothing.

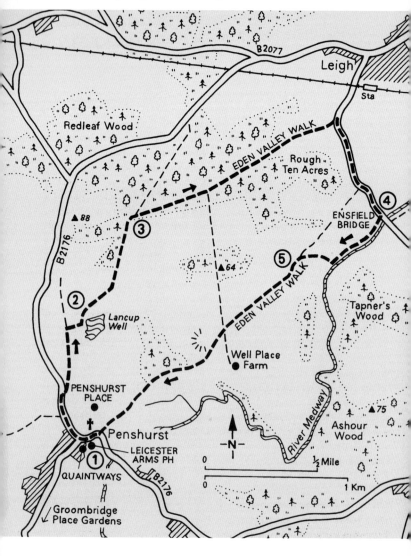

Walk 47 Directions

Walk 47

① Walk up the main street of the village, then turn up the road opposite **Quaintways** tea room. Turn right at a public footpath sign and cross a stile. There are great views of **Penshurst Place** almost immediately and it's well worth a taking a photo. The house dates back to 1341 and the Great Hall is a fabulous example of medieval architecture. It has a timber roof, a musicians' gallery and an open hearth at its centre. There have been some notable visitors to the house over the years: Elizabeth I danced here with Robert Edward Dudley; the Black Prince ate a Christmas dinner here, and the children of Charles I came here after their father was executed. Now walk to a squeeze gate, cross the road, then go through another squeeze gate. Bear to the right in the direction of the lake. Go through one more squeeze gate and, keeping the lake to your right, walk around it then head towards the trees.

> **WHAT TO LOOK FOR** ℹ️
> In Penshurst village, look out for the 'original' **Leicester Square**, named after the Elizabethan Earl of Leicester. The square is enclosed by timbered and tile-hung Tudor cottages.

② The path now veers to the left and goes uphill. Go through two more squeeze gates, then follow the signs for the **Eden Valley Walk** which leads to the right. This is a 15 mile (24km) linear walk that traces the route of the Eden from Edenbridge to Tonbridge.

③ Cross a stile and keep walking ahead along a wide, grassy track lined with trees. It's so atmospheric that you half expect a Royalist soldier to come cantering past you at any moment. At the end of the track cut down to the right and continue along a busy road to reach a sign for the **Eden Valley Walk** on the right-hand side, just before a bridge.

> **WHILE YOU'RE THERE** ℹ️
> A few miles south of Penshurst are **Groombridge Place Gardens**, well known as the setting for the film *The Draughtsman's Contract* (1982). Set in a valley there are lovely water gardens and walks through an area known as the Enchanted Forest. The house itself has been attributed to Wren.

④ Go through a squeeze gate and walk through pastureland, along the side of the **River Medway** which is on your left. Walk by the river for about ¼ mile (400m), then turn right, away from the water, and head across the pasture to a little bridge. Follow the footpath uphill to a stile which takes you on to a concrete track. Turn right and then left at a junction.

⑤ Continue walking ahead, go through a gate, then down to a stile. Bear left and walk down a track from where there are lovely views of **Penshurst Place**. Walk under an archway, then turn right and walk back to the village.

> **WHERE TO EAT AND DRINK** ℹ️
> **Quaintways** is a lovely tea room with lots of character, in the centre of the village. They do very good traditional cakes and scones, as well as light lunches such as sandwiches and soups. They're used to walkers and are very helpful, but if it's been very muddy they do ask you to remove your boots or stick your feet in a couple of plastic bags before going inside.

Walk 48

Royal Passion at Hever

Memories of Henry VIII and Anne Boleyn on this circular walk..

•DISTANCE•	3½ miles (5.7km)
•MINIMUM TIME•	2hrs
•ASCENT / GRADIENT•	279ft (85m) ▲▲▲
•LEVEL OF DIFFICULTY•	👫 👫 👫
•PATHS•	Paths, grassy tracks and field edges, some roads, 6 stiles
•LANDSCAPE•	Woodland and open fields
•SUGGESTED MAP•	aqua3 OS Explorer 147 Sevenoaks & Tonbridge
•START / FINISH•	Grid reference: TQ 476448
•DOG FRIENDLINESS•	Plenty of sections where they can run free
•PARKING•	Car park by Hever Castle
•PUBLIC TOILETS•	At car park

BACKGROUND TO THE WALK

Forget Posh and Becks, Burton and Taylor, even Edward and Mrs Simpson; as celebrity couples go you really can't beat the romance and tragedy of the relationship between Henry VIII and Anne Boleyn. This walk seems to remind you of them with every step, for it starts right next to Hever Castle, Anne's home and the place where the courtship took place.

Henry and Anne Bullen, as she was then, first met at court, where Anne was Lady-in-Waiting to the Queen, Catherine of Aragon. Anne was a sophisticated woman who had spent much of her life in France, and she soon caught the eye of a young nobleman Lord Henry Percy. However, the King disapproved of the match and Anne was sent home to Hever, where she was locked in her room so that she couldn't communicate with her lover. Her father sent her overseas, perhaps in the hope that she'd meet a suitable young man at a foreign court. Sadly for Anne she didn't, and when she returned to Hever in 1525 she found that her father was swamped with honours from the King, largely as recompense for the fact that both Mary, his eldest daughter, and (it was whispered) his wife had become Henry's mistresses.

Henry, desperate for a male heir and looking for a new lover, now turned his attentions to Anne, with whom he rapidly became obsessed. She was fashionable and vivacious and made other women look rather dowdy. She also had an extra finger on her left hand – which her enemies said was a sign that she was a sorceress. Henry began to visit her at Hever, turning up unannounced with a vast entourage of servants and advisers, which he expected his hosts to feed and entertain.

Some say Anne was ambitious and refused to become the King's mistress because she wanted to be queen. Others suggest it would have been extremely difficult to repel Henry's advances. He proposed in 1527 but Anne declined – he was still married. Henry became keener and, in defiance of the Pope, divorced his wife and established the Church of England. He married Anne, who was now pregnant and she changed her name to the regal sounding Boleyn. She gave birth to a daughter, later to become Elizabeth I. She suffered several miscarriages and Henry, more desperate than ever for a son, became furious and claimed Anne had bewitched him. He had her imprisoned, accusing her of adultery with five men – even her own brother. She was found guilty of treason and beheaded on 19th May 1536. Shortly afterwards Henry married Jane Seymour, Anne's Lady-in-Waiting.

Walk 48

Walk 48 Directions

① Walk under the lychgate and go through the churchyard following the **Eden Valley Walk**. The path goes downhill, across a bridge and soon becomes a narrow lane parallel to the road, offering occasional glimpses of the lake at **Hever Castle**. It might look as if it has always been here, yet it was created by William Waldorf Astor when he bought the castle in 1903. The path now bends round, goes through woodland, across another bridge and finally opens out.

② When you come to a house, climb a gate following the **Eden Valley Walk** (which you now follow all the way to Point ④). Pass another house then take the track on the right-hand side. This winds round the edge of the meadow to woodland. When you come to a tarmac road, cross it and pop over a stile.

WHAT TO LOOK FOR

The magnificent gardens at **Hever** appear to date back to Tudor times, yet they were created at the beginning of the 20th century when William Waldorf Astor bought the castle. Astor entertained on a lavish scale, and as the castle was too small to house his many guests, he built the 'Tudor' village to accommodate them.

③ Continue along this enclosed track, which can get very muddy, crossing two more stiles and gradually heading uphill. Another stile leads you past deer fencing and through a gate on to the tarmac road at **Hill Hoath**.

④ Now turn back to the right and go through the large gate, so that you seem to be doubling back on yourself. This takes you on to a broad, grassy track, which is lovely and bouncy to stroll along. Walk ahead (don't be tempted into crossing the stile on the left) and walk up between the trees, passing a lake down on your left-hand side. You soon enter much thicker woodland and the track becomes narrower, but is still clear to follow.

WHERE TO EAT AND DRINK

The **Henry VIII** pub in Hever serves food and the castle itself has tea rooms. If you're visiting the castle, and the weather's good, you could pack a picnic to eat in a quiet spot in the grounds.

⑤ At a branching of footpaths, bear right. Be warned, this can be exceptionally muddy at times. Continue down this track, passing another two areas of woodland until you come to a road.

⑥ Turn right here and walk to **Wilderness Farm**, then take the road that leads to the left opposite the farm. At another road turn right and walk up, past a road that leads to the right. Continue ahead to take the footpath on the right that runs alongside the **Greyhound** pub.

⑦ When you come to a fork by two stiles turn left, then walk around the edge of the field and past a pond. Continue ahead to a lane, where you turn left then take the footpath on the right. Follow this back into **Hever**.

WHILE YOU'RE THERE

If you're a bird lover you might want to visit the bird reserve at nearby **Bough Beech reservoir**. Several rare species have been spotted here over the years, including a Radde's warbler and a little crake. There's also a chance of seeing sandpipers, redstarts, terns and curlews.

Round the Chiding Stone

A loop around Chiddingstone, home of the Chiding Stone.
See map and information panel for Walk 48

Walk 49

•DISTANCE•	1½ miles (2.4km)
•MINIMUM TIME•	1hr
•ASCENT / GRADIENT•	164ft (50m)
•LEVEL OF DIFFICULTY•	

Walk 49 Directions (Walk 48 option)

Chiddingstone is a tiny, picture book Tudor village owned by the National Trust. Close to the village is a large boulder, known as the Chiding Stone, which seems to have served various purposes over the centuries. The Saxons were said to have used it as a boundary, while Druids used it as an altar. By medieval times it was the place to which villagers came to air their grievances in public, complaining perhaps about the behaviour of their neighbours. The wrongdoer would be admonished or 'chided'. Apparently Henry VIII's last wife, Catherine Parr, once lived in the village, in the house next to the inn.

From Point ④ walk ahead, pass the picturesque cottages, turn right at the end of the short lane, then bear left to walk between farm buildings, passing two cottages on your left. Walk past a pond, come up to a gate, Point Ⓐ, and walk across the centre of the field, heading up to the brow of the hill. You'll see **Chiddingstone church** peering down on you. Go through a kissing gate and come on to the road. Turn right along the road and before the lychgate turn down the wide track to your left. This soon skirts around a cottage then bears round the side of the woods down to a bridge over the **Eden**, Point Ⓑ.

Continue ahead, then turn off to climb a stile on the right and continue over the field to another stile. Bear right here, crossing another stile before you join the track and come on to the road, Point Ⓒ. Cross the road, continue along the track ahead and then hop over a stile and go into a wooded area. Walk down to the bottom of a field, where you take the track to the right across two fields and over a stile to reach pretty **Vexour Bridge**, Point Ⓓ.

Turn left to cross the bridge, then go up the drive to **Vexour**. The right of way takes you past Vexour, then bears diagonally right past a pond. Join a wide track, which brings you on to the road. Turn left here and walk down, then take the footpath on the right at the sign for **Weller's Town**. Cross four stiles before reaching a patch of woodland. Walk through this, then join a wide grassy track, which brings you back to the gate. Bear left to walk back to the cottages at **Hill Hoath** and rejoin the Walk 48 at Point ④.

Walk 50

Storming Round Toy's Hill

You'll see many reminders of the Great Storm of 1987 on this short walk.

•DISTANCE•	3 miles (4.8km)
•MINIMUM TIME•	2hrs 15min
•ASCENT / GRADIENT•	98ft (30m) ▲▲▲
•LEVEL OF DIFFICULTY•	🚶 🚶 🚶
•PATHS•	Well-signed woodland paths, 7 stiles
•LANDSCAPE•	Ancient woodland, with views stretching across the Weald
•SUGGESTED MAP•	aqua3 OS Explorer 147 Sevenoaks & Tonbridge
•START / FINISH•	Grid reference: TQ 469517
•DOG FRIENDLINESS•	Good, lots of smells but will need to be kept on lead
•PARKING•	Toy's Hill car park
•PUBLIC TOILETS•	Emmetts Garden

Walk 50 Directions

Toy's Hill is the highest point in Kent and a beautiful area of woodland, owned by the National Trust. The area was devastated by the hurricane or 'Great Storm' of 1987, which ripped through southern England in the early hours of 16th October. The Met Office famously failed to predict the storm. A trainee meteorologist called Anita thought that she'd spotted a hurricane on its way and rang the London Weather Centre to see if they had noticed it. They hadn't. BBC weatherman Bill Giles said that it would be 'breezy in the Channel' and that evening on the BBC TV Forecast, Michael Fish reassured Anita with the words: 'don't worry, there won't be a hurricane'. But there was – and 18 people died. During the night a staggering 15 million trees in the south were uprooted, some of them up to 400 years old. The landscape was changed forever.

Start at the left-hand corner of the car park and follow the signs for **Octavia's Well**. It is named after Octavia Hill, one of the founders of the National Trust, who had it sunk for the villagers in the 19th century. Prior to that they had to collect water in buckets from the Puddledock stream. Follow the track through the woods. You soon enjoy panoramic views over the Weald of Kent. The term Weald is derived from the Andredsweald, the name the Anglo-Saxons gave to the extensive, thick woodlands that once covered a large part of Kent. The Great Storm was responsible for opening up the woodland to reveal these views. One of the reasons so many trees were lost is

---

WHILE YOU'RE THERE ⓘ

Knole House, the largest private house in England, is a mixture of medieval and Jacobean architecture and was the birthplace of Vita Sackville-West. It is owned by the National Trust and is full of fine furnishings that once graced royal palaces such as Whitehall, Kensington and Hampton Court. The house is surrounded by a vast expanse of parkland where deer graze.

WHAT TO LOOK FOR ℹ️

You pass **Emmetts Garden** on this route and it is well worth a visit. It was created in the late 19th century by the banker Frederick Lubbock and is now owned by the National Trust. The garden has plenty of mature trees and rare shrubs, including camellias, magnolias, Japanese maples and ginkgos.

because the storm occurred in October, when the leaves were still on the trees, presenting a greater resistance to the wind. In addition, the ground was waterlogged and the roots of the trees did not have a secure hold in the ground.

Turn left at the waymarker and, in a short distance when the track divides, take the right fork. Pass through a barrier and enter a large grassed area. A tree planted here celebrated the late Queen Mother's 100th Birthday (and Toy's Hill's 80th). Follow the track as it branches to the left, and go down steps to **Puddledock Lane**. Turn left, cross the road and walk down **Scords Lane**.

Pass the house called **Little Chart** on your right, after which your route becomes a track, then widens and bears left along a bridleway leading into **Scords Wood**. This area of woodland is famed for its thick carpet of bluebells in the spring. At the post in the middle of the bridleway, take the right-hand path. When the track splits, turn

WHERE TO EAT AND DRINK ℹ️

You've got lots of choice on this walk. In Ide Hill village there's the popular tea house and coffee shop at the **Elan Arts Centre,** which offers soup, sandwiches and good cakes. For a beer or a bar meal try the **Cock Inn.** There's also a tea room at **Emmetts Garden.**

right and continue to another marker post. On your way there are good views of **Bough Beech reservoir**. Around 60 species of bird breed here each year and it's a great place to see wildfowl such as teal and goosander, and wading birds like the green sandpiper.

Take the track that bears right, cross a stile and turn left. Walk along the top edge of this field, nip over another stile, then bear right and head for a gap in the tree line, where you cross another stile. Make for the bottom right-hand corner of the field and go over a footbridge. Turn left and walk up the left-hand side of the field. Your way now takes you over two more stiles and up into the village of **Ide Hill**.

With the green on your right, walk through the village and fork left to pass in front of the **Cock Inn**. When the road ends continue ahead along a track, cross a stile in the hedgerow on to a lane. Turn left and, when you reach the road, turn right and walk towards **Ide Hill Cricket Club**. Take a footpath on the left and follow it to **Emmetts Garden**.

Take the track that runs to the side of the toilets into the woods. Cross a stile and at a crossing of tracks turn left. Continue ahead at two more track crossings, passing a wooden barrier on your left. Bear right at the next crossing and continue. Go left just before the path climbs sharply upwards and continue until you come back to the car park. There's a sign in this part of the woods letting you know that the area has been deliberately left untouched after the storm of 1987. You can see natural regeneration taking place as saplings spring up in the cleared areas.

Walking in Safety

All these walks are suitable for any reasonably fit person, but less experienced walkers should try the easier walks first. Route finding is usually straightforward, but you will find that an Ordnance Survey map is a useful addition to the route maps and descriptions.

Risks

Although each walk here has been researched with a view to minimising the risks to the walkers who follow its route, no walk in the countryside can be considered to be completely free from risk. Walking in the outdoors will always require a degree of common sense and judgement to ensure that it is as safe as possible.

- Be particularly careful on cliff paths and in upland terrain, where the consequences of a slip can be very serious.

- Remember to check tidal conditions before walking on the seashore.

- Some sections of route are by, or cross, busy roads. Take care and remember traffic is a danger even on minor country lanes.

- Be careful around farmyard machinery and livestock, especially if you have children with you.

- Be aware of the consequences of changes in the weather and check the forecast before you set out. Carry spare clothing and a torch if you are walking in the winter months. Remember the weather can change very quickly at any time of the year, and in moorland and heathland areas, mist and fog can make route finding much harder. Don't set out in these conditions unless you are confident of your navigation skills in poor visibility. In summer remember to take account of the heat and sun; wear a hat and carry spare water.

- On walks away from centres of population you should carry a whistle and survival bag. If you do have an accident requiring the emergency services, make a note of your position as accurately as possible and dial 999.

Acknowledgements

Rebecca Ford would like to thank the National Trust and Kent Wildlife Trust for the information they provided. Special thanks should go to Edward Longbottom, Fiona Ballantyne and, above all, Billy O'Reilly, for accompanying me through Kent's muddy fields. Thanks too to Mum and Dad for all the hot dinners, hot baths – and plasters.

AA Publishing and Outcrop Publishing Services would like to thank Chartech for supplying aqua3 maps for this book. For more information visit their website: www.aqua3.com.

Series management: Outcrop Publishing Services Ltd, Cumbria
Series editor: Chris Bagshaw
Front cover: AA Photo Library